Lettering for Embroidery

Lettering for Embroidery

Pat Russell

B.T. Batsford Limited, London

First published 1971
Second impression 1985
ISBN 0 7134 5034 7

Filmset by Keyspools Ltd, Golborne, Lancashire
Printed in Spain by Jerez Industrial, S.A.
for the publishers
B. T. Batsford Limited, 4 Fitzhardinge Street, London W IH OAH

Contents

1 Trinity Frontal, Alban-Neve Centre for the Deaf, Luton. Pat Russell and Elizabeth Ward

Introduction

Many designers may feel that letter forms and lettering are irrelevant to their work and will feel no inclination to make use of them, but others will recognise in lettering a fascinating source of design and will wish to use it both for its decorative possibilities and for its semantic significance.

The uses of lettering in embroidery can be divided roughly into three categories: lettering for information, lettering for decoration, and lettering used as a basis for an abstract design. These categories will not, of course, be watertight compartments and will be found to overlap in many cases, but the design approach for each will be subtly different.

The first group includes lettering used on formal embroideries such as banners, where the main purpose of the lettering is to convey information. While, of course, it may also be decorative, and must in any case form an integral part of the design, it would be defeating its objective if the letters were not easily readable. It follows that such lettering will have to bear close similarity to letter forms in everyday use; the type of lettering that we see around us, in books, newspapers, on hoardings, and on all the other occasions where lettering conveys information. Therefore, embroidered letters in this first category will of necessity have to resemble closely their typographic counterparts, being adapted only to suit their own particular medium of embroidery.

The second category, letters as decoration, could of course, cover all embroidered lettering, but it particularly refers to letters used primarily as ornament. While the lettering should be decipherable, legibility is not its prime function. Such lettering may also be used on formal embroideries and on all occasions where letters are used as a decorative pattern. The fact that it also contains a 'message' in the literary sense only serves to give it added interest. Lettering as decoration in informal embroideries covers a very wide field, limited only by the craftsman's imagination and ingenuity: cyphers and monograms of all sorts (although these may also be used in formal work), words or initials used as decorative motifs on clothing for both adults and children, or on household articles such as cushion covers, table cloths, napkins, napkin rings, etc.

In the third category, letters are used as a springboard or starting point for designs which, in their final form, will bear very little reference to their letter form origins. Here the designer may select certain letters and then, by experiment, analyse and develop their design characteristics, retaining some parts and rejecting others, arranging, adapting and re-organising until a lively and satisfactory composition is achieved. The potential of letter forms as a source of inspiration for design can be investigated in much the same way as designs are developed from any other natural or mechanical forms.

One of the main difficulties encountered by the beginner when considering lettering for use in designs, is that it is a subject with which he is much too familiar! From early school days, letters in the form of reading and writing have been thrust upon him; not a day goes by when he does not have to make use of them in one form or another. The endless permutations and combinations of the twenty six letters are perpetually displayed before him, conveying messages of every description: instruction, advice, information, stories, ideas, poetry, statements, laws, facts. But almost always, it is the literary content of the lettering that has concerned him, he has either been conveying or assimilating information. Seldom has he stopped to consider, to look at or to examine the form of the letters in detail. It is this *look* of the letter that becomes so important when it is considered as an element of design. The eye must be trained afresh to see letters as design motifs and to assess the value of lettering in aesthetic terms. It takes time and not a little perseverance to learn to view letters in this way.

It can be a help to look first at some lettering in unfamiliar form: Greek lettering 5 (though not, of course, to the Greek scholar) may perhaps be more readily appreciated in terms of pattern and design as there is not so much temptation to try and read the words, although the familiarity of some of the letter forms may hinder a purely visual approach. Perhaps Chinese or Arabic characters provide a better example. The Chinese character 6 in the embroidery illustrated here can easily be accepted as abstract pattern, a decorative motif in its own right, taking its appointed place and harmonising with the richness of the other elements of the design: the flowing and unfamiliar pattern of the Arabic letters in the appliqué panel forms a readily appreciable abstract design of interrelated lines and 8 curves. Unfamiliar lettering can be recognised as being in fact lettering by the abstract nature of the component parts and by a certain consciousness of a random repetition of motifs or of parts of motifs, indicating that this is indeed a sign language, conveying a message to those who understand the significance of the symbols.

2　Cloak of Henry II of Germany. Reproduced by courtesy of Bamberg Textilienmuseum. Copyright Hirmer Verlag, Munich

3 Chimney hanging, Leipzig 1577. Reproduced by courtesy of the Städt Museum des Kunsthandwerks, Leipzig

4 The Sandham Memorial Chapel at Burghclere is famed for its murals by Stanley Spencer. Somewhat overshadowed by these is a most interesting altar frontal of white linen embroidered with fish motifs, drawn thread work and lettering in white and pale gold. The lettering is in the form of a lattice. On the horizontal bands a quotation from the Bible I AM THE RESURRECTION AND THE LIFE HE THAT On the vertical bands a quotation from Shakespeare WE ARE SUCH STUFF AS DREAMS ARE MADE ON AND OUR LITTLE The lettering is in pale gold in a slightly condensed form of the classical Roman letter

6 Chinese embroidered lettering. Crown copyright. Reproduced by courtesy of the Trustees of the Victoria and Albert Museum, London

5 Byzantine embroidery with Greek lettering. Crown copyright. Reproduced by courtesy of the Trustees of the Victoria and Albert Museum, London

7 Preliminary design for a panel based on letters and symbol of the sign of the Zodiac *Pisces*. Catherine V. Theaker, third year student, Birmingham College of Art

8 Arabic appliqué lettering. Crown copyright. Reproduced by courtesy of the Trustees of the Victoria and Albert Museum, London

When letters are really looked at, and all their subtle details noted, it may appear an almost impossible task to sort out and classify their seemingly endless variations. Letter forms in general use in the West today have been developing over the last two thousand years, so it is not surprising that their infinite variety is confusing. Indeed the more this fascinating subject is investigated, the more complex it appears and the more formidable may seem the task undertaken in embarking on the use of lettering in designs at all! The object of chapters 1 to 7 of this book is to try and set up some signposts to help find ways through this maze of letter forms. An attempt has been made to establish some fundamental principles of letter design by discussing the basic construction of letters, the formation of alphabets, the assembly of letters to form words, and of words to make the 'message', the integrating of the wording with the whole composition. These basic principles can be applied to lettering whatever its medium and so should, it is hoped, interest all craftsmen who need to use lettering in their work. Chapters 8 to 17 of the book relate the design of letters and lettering specifically to the craft of embroidery and shows how letters may be developed and adapted for this particular medium.

Acknowledgment

The task of compiling this book was made all the more pleasant by the interest and encouragement of many friends and colleagues who helped so generously. Especial thanks are due to the staff of the Embroidery Department of the Victoria and Albert Museum, London, and to Dr Hassall at the Bodleian Library, Oxford; to the staffs and students of the Schools of Embroidery at Birmingham College of Art and Design, at Goldsmiths College of Art, London and at the Manchester Polytechnic; to Eirian Short, Kathleen Norris, Kathleen Whyte, Isabelle Chapman, Charlotte Cope, Cynthia Kendzior and Pru Russell for supplying so readily examples of their work; to Joan H. Koslan Schwartz, Virginia, USA for her interesting contributions; to Jane Dorman for her assistance; to Mr K. L. Bassett of Bernina Sewing Machines Limited for his helpful cooperation; to my mother for reading and correcting proofs for me; to Mary Baker for her welcome help; and most gratefully to Ian Ross for photographing the work so well and so willingly.

Abingdon 1971   P.R.

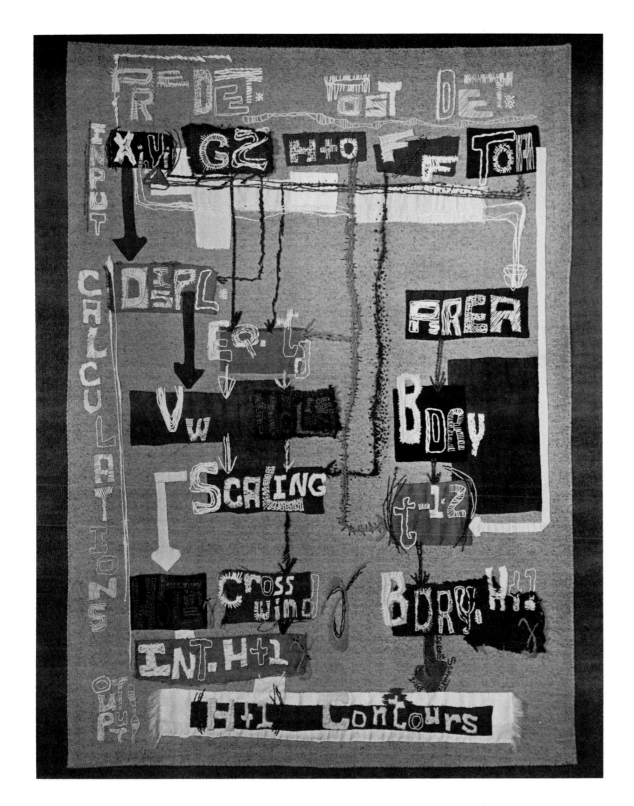

9 *Preface*. An expression of a flow chart for a computer programme. This banner was designed and worked by Joan H. Koslan Schwartz in 1968 to celebrate a scientist. It is now in the Collection of Dr Benjamin L. Schwartz, McLean, Virginia, USA, by courtesy of whom it is reproduced

10 Fish and bird letters from early tenth century
French manuscripts. Bodleian Library

1 Basic construction and design of individual letters

In considering the design and construction of letters, two questions should be asked: firstly, 'What is a letter?' and secondly, 'What is a "good" letter?'

WHAT IS A LETTER?

A letter can be described as a symbol consisting of a recognisable arrangement of straight lines and curves. An I is a vertical line; an H two vertical lines joined by a horizontal line; an A two sloping lines meeting in a point at the top and joined by a horizontal crossbar; an O is a circle; a P, a vertical line with a curved line starting from the top on the right of the vertical and rejoining the vertical at some point further down—when this curved line meets the vertical at its base, the letter becomes a D and therefore no longer reads as a P.

It is an interesting exercise to experiment in drawing letters in skeleton form (ie by single strokes and making the letter in its simplest form) in as many ways as possible, thus proving for one's self what an enormous variety of letters can be made and how many of them are easily recognisable. In making skeleton letters, it should be noted that I not I, J not J and G not G are the simplest form of each of these letters; in the second version of each, the small horizontal strokes are decorative additions and not part of the basic letter form.

11 Basic letter forms

12a

12b

13   Roman capital **E**

WHAT IS A GOOD LETTER?

A good letter may be said to be one in which the arrangement of lines, or lines and curves, is recognisable as making up the given letter; one in which the strokes are well-proportioned in their relationship one with another; and one in which they are so organised that their composition stands as a valid decorative unit in its own right. Further, in a wider context, a letter cannot be said to be good unless it is suitable in size, design and character to the particular purpose and environment for which it is intended, and its form is appropriate to the tools and materials used.

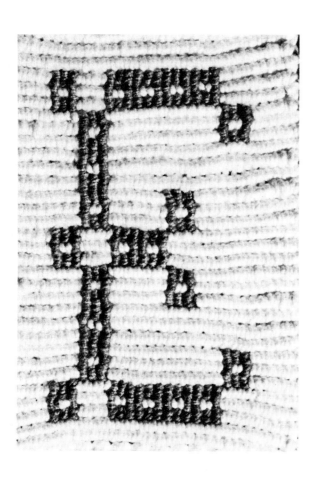

14   Letter **E** in a type of macramé known as Cavandoli work. The decorative form of the letter is appropriate to and arises from the technique used. Eirian Short

15   Letters formed with free machine embroidery techniques. Pat Russell

16 Motorway sign showing lettering suitable in size, design and character to the purpose for which it is used

17 Sketch design for an engraved glass font about 406 mm (16 in.) high by David Peace showing lettering suitable for its purpose and for the tools and materials

NN
NNNNI

A
A
A
A
A
A
I

18 Versions of N and A showing exaggerated distortion

19 Detail of lettering from German PIETA

Further consideration of the letters on the experimental sheet, figure 12, will show that too much exaggeration in any direction will eventually make the letters unreadable and that therefore there is a limit to the amount of distortion that can be acceptable. For example, if the N is made narrower and narrower, the diagonal will eventually fuse with the vertical and the letter will be indistinguishable from an I. Similarly if the A is widened and widened it will eventually become a horizontal line.

Looking at the sheet, it can be seen that some letters are indeed 'better looking' than others, their combination of strokes more balanced and more happily proportioned, producing satisfying letters forms, while other arrangements are ill-balanced producing awkward or even absurd looking letters.

Some letters have unhappy, flabby looking curves while in others they are strong and sprightly. The proportions of the horizontal to the vertical lines in some are dull or out of scale, in others the proportions appear satisfying and 'just right'. Some look as if they might topple over at any minute, others may look incomplete, as though part of the letter had

20

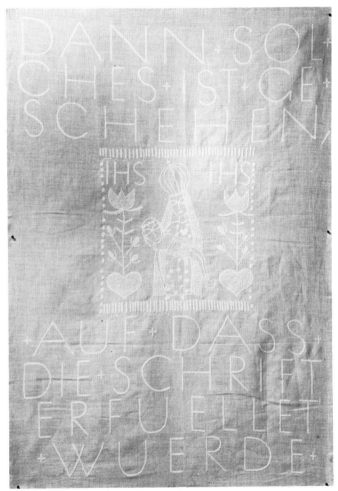

21   German PIETA in whitework

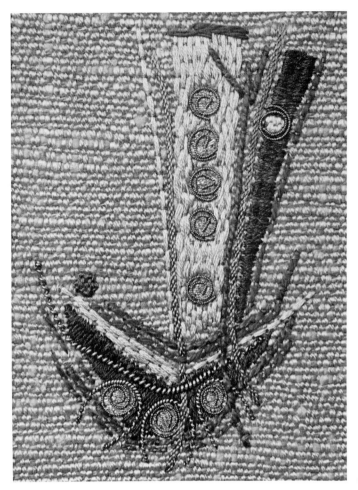

22   Letter **J** worked by Kathleen Norris

23

been amputated. It is only by considering each letter and deciding whether it is a satisfactory abstract motif in itself, or whether it can be improved in any way, that one can assess its value aesthetically and decide whether it is a good letter or not. In the end, the decision must be a personal one, but by training oneself to 'look' at letters and continually to assess them as individual abstract design forms, the eye can be trained to select that which is vigorous and true and to reject the weak and the false. In the same way these principles can be applied to more complex letter forms.

19

The simplest of letter forms are subject to many and complex variations, the three main categories being:

1 Variation in the weight of the stroke (ie the proportion of thickness of stroke to height of letter).
2 The use of serifs.
3 The use of thick and thin strokes in the same letter.

23 1 The thickness of the stroke in proportion to the height of the letter will give a heavy or light looking letter depending on that proportion. It should be noted that taken to extremes, this can make the letter either completely indecipherable or disappear altogether. There is therefore a practical limit to the thickness or thinness of stroke used in a letter of a given height. This can readily be seen by considering the letter E, which consists of a vertical stroke and three horizontal strokes. The thickness of the stroke must be something less than one third of the height of the letter, otherwise the spaces between the horizontal strokes will disappear and the letter become a solid rectangle, thus completely obliterating the letter form. A good standard letter will result when the thickness of the stroke is one tenth to one eighth the height of the letter.

24 2 A serif is the small extension at the beginning or end of a stroke. This can be very simple in form, originally arising from the use of pen or chisel in making the letter, or it can be elaborated, adding a positive, decorative feature to the letter.

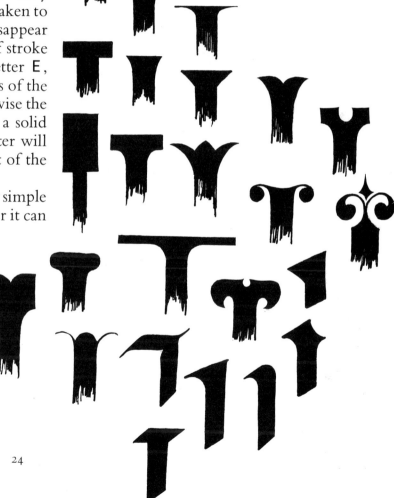

23

24

LONDON

HENRY

OBS

SUNDAY

SAINT

MERIT

TRACE

SELFRIDGES

25   Everyday type faces

3   In most type faces used in books and newspapers today, and in nearly all formal lettering, there is a variation in the thickness of the stroke, the vertical strokes tending to be thick and the horizontals thin, and in the curved letters, a gradual swelling and contracting of the stroke from thin to thick, to thin again. This can be sometimes in exaggerated form: at other times only the most subtle variations are apparent. This use of thick and thin strokes in the same letter is usually, but not necessarily always, combined with the use of a serif. This type of letter is generally known as 'Roman' and will be discussed in greater detail in Chapter 3.

26   Indecipherable letter. German fifteenth century

27a–c   Embroidered letters based on nineteenth century decorative letters

27a   Quilted cushion letter **K** based on nineteenth century typeface

24

In some ornate letter forms, the thick strokes, and sometimes even the thin strokes, are patterned and elaborated, sometimes to the extent of almost defeating their usefulness as letters. These decorated letters were much in vogue in the nineteenth century, reflecting the Victorian love of pattern and complexity, and today they are enjoying a certain revival. In the right setting they can be most effective and the embroiderer will find their whole-hearted exuberance and wealth of imaginative detail well worth studying and a rewarding source of ideas. Early manuscripts too have their ornamental capitals, with complex interlacing of ribbon-like strokes and abundance of decorative detail. Thus it can be seen that capital letters alone present us with infinite variations, nearly all of which are readable and most of them easily so. It is a remarkable tribute to the quality of perception of the human mind and eye, that letters are instantly recognisable in such complex variety of forms: and this point is emphasised in the enormous difficulties encountered in the designing of a computer that can read any form of text and not only the special letters designed for the purpose.

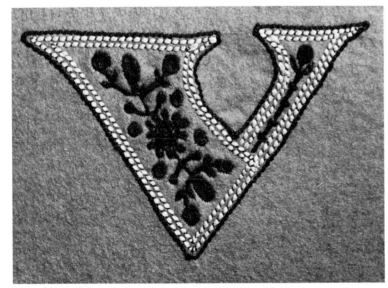

27b V Cable stitch with stranded embroidery cotton on spool of machine. Eirian Short

27c I Counted thread. Back stitch, half-cross stitch, cross stitch, brick stitch. Cynthia Kendzior

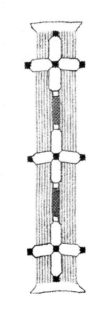

27c

28 Varieties of letter M

S
QVI
HOD
ER
NA
DIE
PER
UNIGENI

tum tuum aeternitatis nobis aditum deuicta
morte referasti· uota nra quae preuenendo af
spiras &iam adiuuando prosequere· pereund.

31 Part of heading of First Charter of Abingdon
1556. Interlaced capitals

◄ 29 Late tenth century illumination showing cross and alpha and omega. Bodleian Library

◄ 30 Decorative initial from German ninth century manuscript. Bodleian Library

32 Decorative letters. Seventeenth, eighteenth and nineteenth centuries

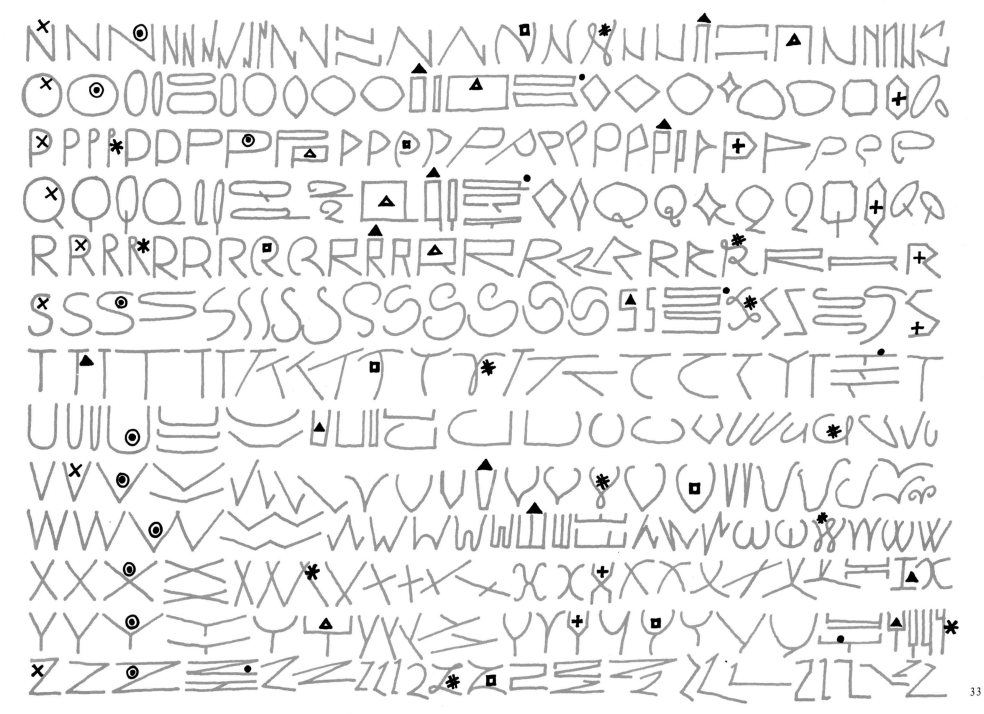

33

2 Basic design of an alphabet

³³ On examining the pages of experimental skeleton letters, it can be seen that certain letters in each group have some sort of similarity: the very narrow A goes with the very narrow B, C, etc; the wide letters go together, the slanting match up as do the 'low' or the 'high' waisted; the 'square' O goes with the square topped P and B . It is this basic similarity that makes a letter belong to its own particular alphabet. All the letters in one alphabet will bear a certain family resemblance to each other.

To develop this further, it is necessary to examine an alphabet in a simple form and to divide it up into 'family groups' of related letters. O C D G Q are all based on the curve and proportions of the letter O and form one main group. Other letters with

³⁴ curves are B P R S and these form a related group, based roughly on the curves found in two small Os placed one on top of the other. E F L I go together and H can be said to go with U and N as each letter has two strong verticals. The letters with diagonals form another group and it is easy to see the relationship between A V M W, while N and Z are their close cousins, and X Y and K not far removed. J can join B P R S but T is a letter apart, although it has a family likeness to E F L I and also to H. In any alphabet, this family resemblance must be respected ensuring as it does a unity and cohesion of design within that alphabet.

³⁵ For example, if the O is made oval or square shaped, the letters in the alphabet with curves must all have the same characteristic. If the stroke of the I is finished with a serif, the terminale of all the other letters must be finished in the same way.

The O and the I may be considered the parent letters in any alphabet, imparting

³⁶ their own particular characteristics to the rest of the family. The I shows the character of the straight lines; their thickness in proportion to the height of the letter; whether they terminate in a serif and if so what form this takes; whether or not they are decorated in any way. Likewise the O shows the form of all the other curves and also indicates whether the letters are 'shaded' (ie whether the letters are built up of thick and thin strokes or whether the strokes are all of the same width). The design of the O will also show the

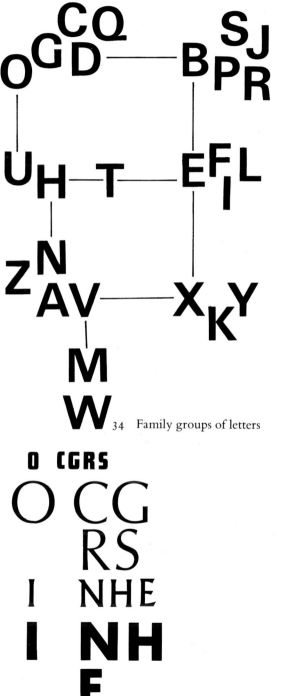

34 Family groups of letters

35 Forms of I and O

29

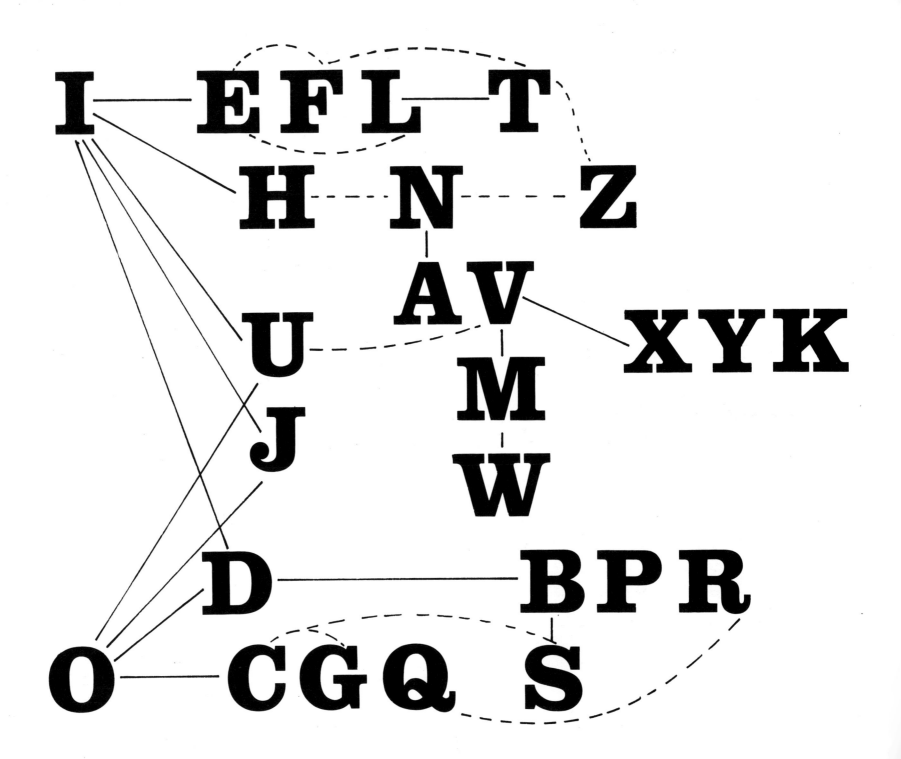

36 Alphabet set out to show family relationships

³⁷ general height to width proportions of the letters of the alphabet; a tall narrow O indicating a condensed characteristic in all the other letters while an O wider than it is high will imply an expanded alphabet.

To belong to the same family, the I and the O must have a certain affinity with each other. This usually means that the width of the stroke of the I and the thick parts ³⁸ of the O are the same, and that any decoration involved is similar.

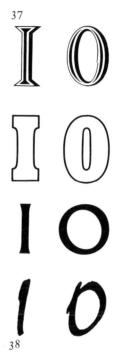

O CNSHT

O CNHT

37

I O

I O

I O

I O

38

39 Shoe bag with sketch of alphabet built up from using identical triangular shapes and straight lines. The triangular pieces of the letters on the shoe bag are sewn down with machine zigzag stitch, reinforced and decorated with matching straight stitching. The straight lines are of lurex braid, sewn down by machine zigzag

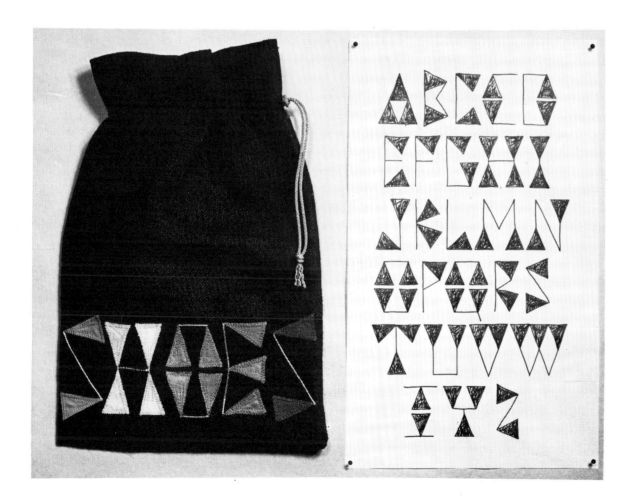

oce il
s jft
a bd
pqg
nhmr
u
vwy
xkz

40 Family grouping of lower case letters

41 Detail from illustrated alphabet panel. The lower case letters are based on pen-made italic forms: the capitals are adapted from a conventional type face. Pat Russell

In discussing alphabets, one must also consider that other branch of the family consisting of the small letters, or *lower case* as it is called. Here the same principal of dividing the alphabet into related groups can be applied and the character of the family retained, the lower case o being nearly always identical to the capital letter O but about half to two thirds its size. Related also is the *italic* branch of the same family, both in capitals and lower case, keeping again all the salient family characteristics but with all the letters sloping to some degree to the right and generally slightly compressed. From the embroiderers point of view it is unlikely that the different branches of the alphabet will be needed in the same piece of work, capitals nearly always being used, but it is well to bear in mind these different variations which may occasionally bring a spice of variety to a piece of work or act as an inspiration for designs.

3 The Roman alphabet

Almost all of the lettering used today has sprung from one particular point, the very fine and sophisticated letter evolved by the Romans during the first century AD. This in its turn came from adapting the earlier Greek letters but, since the first century, the form of letters used in the western world has varied very little; a few letters have been added, J, K and W, and the lower case letters have developed but for design the Roman letter remains unsurpassed. The finest and best known example of this lettering is that found on the Trajan column in Rome (there is a full size cast of it in the Victoria and Albert Museum).

42 Inscription on the Trajan column, Rome, First century AD. Crown copyright. Reproduced by courtesy of the Trustees of the Victoria and Albert Museum, London

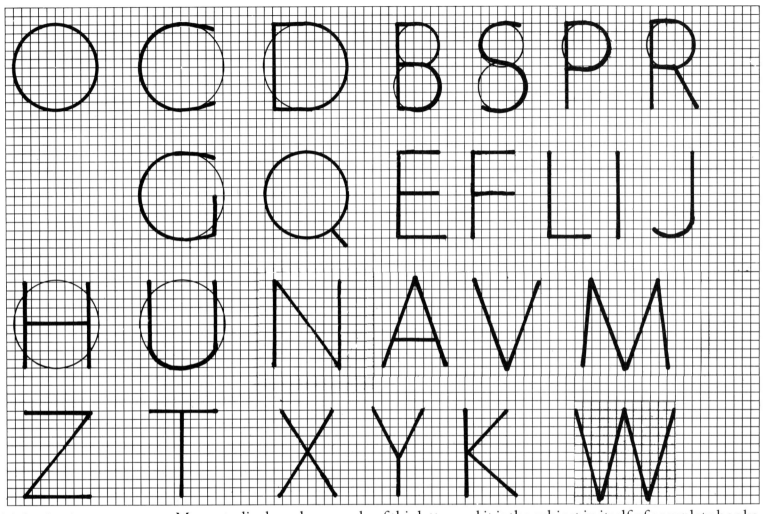

43 Skeleton Roman alphabet showing geometric structure of the letters

Many studies have been made of this letter and it is the subject in itself of complete books, but the for purpose of this book a simplified analysis will suffice.

Being logical and very methodical, the Romans took for their basis an O based on the circle, the C D G and Q all using parts of the same circle.

B and S were based on two circles on top of each other, the lower one being slightly larger than the upper, this being visually more satisfying than using two circles

43

of the same size. With P and R, on the other hand, the bow of the letter takes up slightly more than the top half of the letter, again because this makes for a more balanced look to the letter. In all these letters the D shaped part will be of similar proportions to the D itself. E and F tie up with B , being letters with top and bottom halves; the upper arms of the E and F being approximately equal to half the height of the letter, the lower arm of the E very slightly longer. The proportions of the L are the same as the vertical and lower arm of the E (in practice it is sometimes advisable to make the lower arm a little shorter. See THE SPACES IN BETWEEN Chapter 5, page 45).

H U and N may be made to tie up with the round O by making the area of each letter approximately the same. This gives as a basis for the letter a rectangle whose width is approximately four fifths of its height. This same proportion is used as a basis for the diagonal letters A and V. M is built up from a four-fifths based V with the outer legs sloping slightly outwards. The W did not exist in Trajan times but an appropriate letter can be formed by using two slightly narrower Vs side by side. Z is also formed on this four fifths rectangle. X and Y and K are diagonal letters but also letters with a top and bottom half. This brings them into the category of the narrower letters, but their complex forms demand a rather wider basic structure, the width being about three fifths of the height. J is formed from a vertical and a curve which is similar in shape to the lowest curve of the S. T can be based on the four fifths rectangle but often in practice it is made narrower.

The other important characteristic of the Roman letter is the fact that the letters are built of thick and thin strokes. This probably originated in the use of the square cut pen (either reed or quill) which was used for writing at that time. When used at an angle of about 30° to the horizontal, the square cut pen produces letters with similarly placed thicks and thins. The shading (ie the arrangement of thicks and thins) in the Trajan O is tilted to the left slightly so that the thinnest part of the letter is not at the top and bottom but slightly to the left at the top and to the right at the bottom, exactly the same way as it is positioned in a pen made letter. The proportion of the width of the thick stroke to the height of the letter in Trajan Roman is about one tenth, the thin stroke being approximately one third the width of the thick. This gives a fine and elegant letter. In some later examples, the width of the thick stroke is one eighth of the height, and the thin stroke half the thickness, resulting in a bolder and more rugged letter form.

The terminals of the Trajan Roman letter are finished with a curved and pointed serif

44   Pen-made Roman letters

RGEAN

of refined and elegant proportions. This form of serif arose naturally from the use of the chisel, the tool with which the lettters were made. For this reason also the 'straight' 45 strokes are not straight, as if drawn with a ruler, but have very subtle curves to them, swelling naturally into the serif. It is a point of interest also to notice that the size of the letters used on the Trajan column is not uniform throughout, the lettering being larger at the top than at the base. This is so that, to the viewer, the panel being somewhat above eye level, the letters in perspective will appear all of the same size and is a measure of the care taken by these early craftsmen in the visual quality of their design and of the sophistication of their work.

    Almost all of the printing types in use today are based on, or strongly influenced by, 46 the early Roman letters. Some in fact are almost identical, others take the classical proportions and use them in block letter form (ie the letters are formed throughout of the

46   Modern typefaces based on Roman letter

ABCDEFGHIJKLMNOPQRSTUVWXYZ

ABCDEFGHIJKLMNOPQRSTUVWXYZ

ABCDEFGHIJKLMNOPQRSTUVWXYZ

ABCDEFGHIJKLMNOPQRSTUVWXYZ

ABCDEFGHIJKLMNOPQRSTUVWXYZ

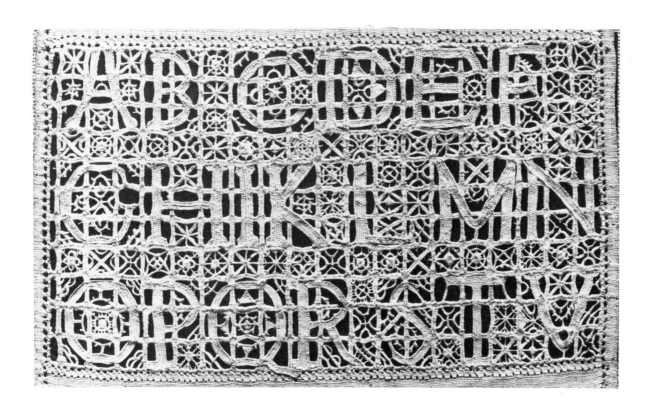

same width of stroke); others vary the proportions of the thicks and thins, or the proportion of stroke width to height. Some again take the shaded characteristic from the Roman but not the classical proportions and use it in letters all of which tend to be of the same width. It would appear that it is only the letters designed for computer consumption that owe nothing to the Roman heritage, and these are to the normal eye most difficult to read. Can the numerals on a cheque book be read with ease? (nevertheless they have a certain decorative quality and it may be that before long, through familiarity, they will become more readily decipherable).

47 Cut and drawn thread work alphabet. English sampler dating from middle of the seventeenth century. The letter forms, except for the letter **E**, follow the classical proportions of the Roman letters. Crown copyright. Reproduced by courtesy of the Trustees of the Victoria and Albert Museum, London

COMPUTER ALPHABET

48

LIBRADIESOMNIQ·PAR
ETMEDIVMLVCIAIQ·VN
EXERCETEVIRIIAVROSS

49 Written Roman square capitals. Fourth or fifth
century (actual size)

OCCIDERENT	ANEAWCIH
ACCEPTUMAUTEM	AABONTECAC
EUM	AYTON
DISCIPULI	OIMAOHTAI
NOCTE	NYKTOC
PERMURUM	AIATOYTIXOYC
DIMISERUNT	KAOHKAN
LAXANTES	XAAACANTEC
INSPORTA	ENCΠYPIAI
CUMUENISSEAUTEM	ΠAPAΓENOMENA
PAULUS	OΠAYAOC
INHIEROSOLYMIS	ENIAHM
·TEMPTABAT	EΠEIPATO
ADHAERERE	KOAAACOAI
DISCIPULIS	TOICMAOHTAIC

50 Written Roman and Greek uncials. Sixth century.
Bodleian Library, Oxford

CREDOINDMPATREM
OMNIPOTEM
ETINXPOIHAFILIUMEIS
ANICAMDOMINOMNOS
TROM QAINATUSEST
DESPASCOETMARIAUIR
GINE QUISUBPONTIOPI
LATOCRACIFIXUSEST
ETSEPULTAS TERTIA
DIERESURREXITAMOR
TUISASCENDITINCAELIS
SEDETADDEXTERAPATRIS
ANDECIENTURUSEST
IUDICAREUIUASETMOR
TUOSETINSPUSCO SCA
ECCLESIAREMISSIONE
PECCATORCUM CARNIS·
RESURRECTIONIS·

51 A freer version of written Roman uncials. Seventh
century. Bodleian Library, Oxford

4 Development of lower case letters

In the early centuries AD, until about the eighth century, all formal writing and lettering was in capitals; the lower case or small letter did not exist. With the spread of learning and the demand for more and more books, (which at this time were all, of course, written by hand) the actual speed of the writing had to be increased. This speeding up process resulted in a quickly written form of the capital letter, the straight lines tending to become curves (Uncials). From this half-uncials (ie a letter form halfway between capitals and lower case) developed and, eventually, by the tenth century the lower case letter very much as we know it today.

49
51
53
54

52   Development from capitals to small letters

53   Irish half-uncial writing. Macregol Gospel, ninth century. Bodleian Library, Oxford

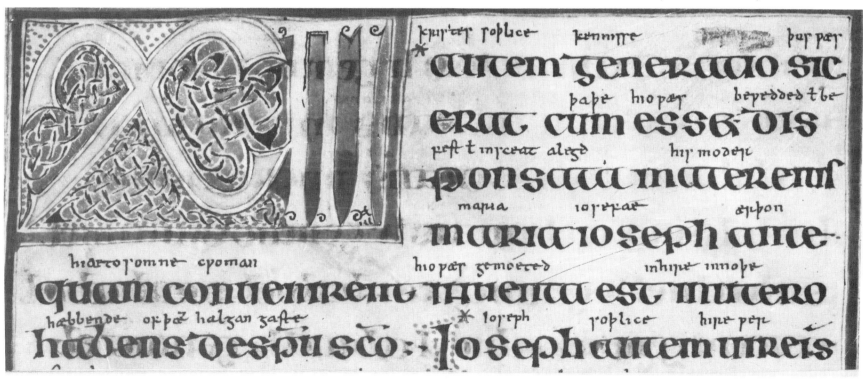

54

40

56

56

54 St Margaret's Gospel. Early eleventh century showing development of lower case letters. Bodleian Library, Oxford

55 Apocalypse. English fourteenth century manuscript. Gothic writing. Bodleian Library, Oxford

56 The Gutenberg Bible. The opening of the First Book of Kings, circa 1456   cf 55

Valerii Maximi Historici Celeberrimi Factorum ac
Dictorum Memorabilium Ad Tiberium Cæsarem Liber Primus Foeliciter Incipit

RBIS ROMAE EXTERArumque gentium facta simul
ac dicta memoratu digna que
apud alios latius diffusa na
runt: q ut breuiter cognosci
possint ab illustribz electa
auctoribz deligere constitui
Vt documēta summe uolenti
bz longe inquisitonis labor
absit. Nec mihi cuncta com
plectendi cupido incessit: m
Q uis enim omnis tui gesta m
modico uoluminū numero comprehēderit? Aut quis com
pos mētis. domesticæ peregrineque historiæ seriem foelici
superiorum stilo conditam: uel attentiore cura: uel prestan

58

PLaciturum tibi esse librū meum suspicabar:tam
q̄ scribis ualde gaudeo.Quod me admones de no
desq; ut meminerim Iouis oratioém quæ est in extrem
uero memini:& illa omnia mihi magis scripsi q̄ cæteris
stridie q̄ tu es profectus multa nocte cum Vibullio uer
Cumq; ego egissem de istis operibus atque inscription
benigne respōdit:magnā spem attulit:cum Crasso se d
mihiq; ut idem facerem persuasit.Crassum consulem e
reduxi:suscæpi rem:dixiq; esse φ Clodius hoc tempore

57   Fifteenth century manuscript from Northern Italy. Open Gothic or
Rotunda hand. Bodleian Library, Oxford

58   Italian Renaissance manuscript, late fifteenth century. Bodleian
Library, Oxford   cf 59

59   Type face designed by Nicolas Jenson. Second half of fifteenth
century   cf 58

After the tenth century, while not altering very much in its basic form, the design of the lower case letter developed in two main streams, one in the South in Italy and one in Germany and Northern Europe. The Italian letter kept very much the open character and classical proportions of the Roman letter. In the North the letter form became compressed and angular and resulted in the highly decorative but somewhat illegible Gothic letter.

The invention of printing in Germany in the first half of the fifteenth century resulted 56 in the earliest books using this Gothic form of letter but later, when the art of printing spread to Italy, the Roman form was retained and today this form is almost universal in the 59 Western world. In Germany, however, and other central European countries the influence of the Gothic is still in evidence.

60   Festival of Britain cushion. Designed by Robert Stewart and worked by Kathleen Whyte

61 Sampler worked by Mary Ann Body, aged 9, in 1789. Crown copyright. Reproduced by courtesy of the Trustees of the Victoria and Albert Museum, London

62 Frontal for St Mark's Chapel, Alban-Neve Centre for the Deaf, Luton. Pat Russell and Elizabeth Ward

5 Spacing: letters into words

Having considered the construction and design of letters as individual design units and their formation into alphabets, the next problem is the arrangement of the letters to form words: for however well designed letters may be, unless their spacing is satisfactory, the total effect will be disappointing. The letter must not be considered only in isolation but as a member of a group of letters that together make up a word.

Much as letters were considered as abstract motifs built up of a given series of straight and curved lines, so words must be looked upon as more complex motifs formed from a given series of letters.

THE SPACES IN BETWEEN

The spaces formed in between the letters are equally important as elements of design as are the letters themselves. This is a fact of fundamental importance and its significance cannot be over-emphasised. By the reader it is easily overlooked, for good spacing is of its very nature unobtrusive, but for the designer, it is of paramount importance and must continuously be kept in mind. It is essential for him to train his eye to look at and assess these spaces in between and to make sure that he gives them equal precedence with the letters in design consideration. An enlightening exercise is to draw, not the letters them-
63 selves, but the spaces that are made between each pair of letters, and to consider these shapes as the design units rather than the letters themselves. This exercise can also be
64 carried out in freely cut paper with interesting results. The importance of these areas will
65 soon come to be remembered and appreciated.

63

64 Duffle bag decorated with words THIS AND THAT by Jane Dorman. The design, seen in foreground, was developed by considering the spaces formed in between the letters and words. These were cut out freely in black paper and arranged in their appropriate order to form a band of pattern. The design was carried out in coloured felts on orange hopsack, sewn down with straight machine stitching

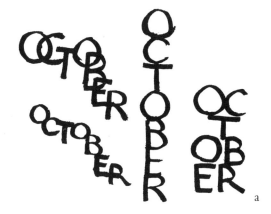

65   Janet Mitchell, first year student, School of Design, Oxford Polytechnic. After some initial experiments with a pen to seek out the design potential of the word OCTOBER (a), one arrangement was chosen and developed (b). From the final design, the letters were cut out and stuck down on contrasting paper to make the positive design (c). The cut away pieces were then freely re-arranged as a further development (d)

47

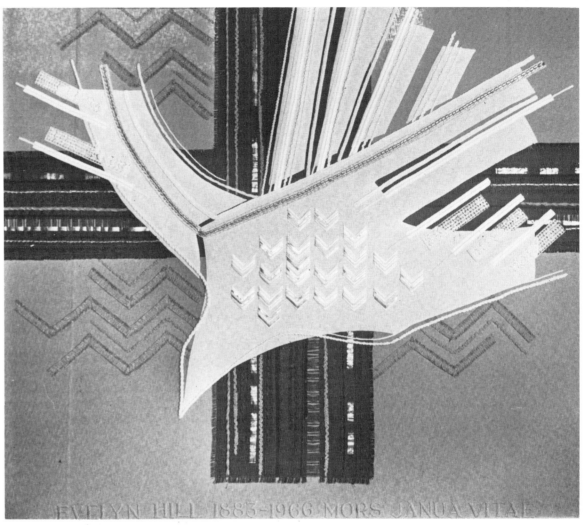

66 Mothers' Union banner for Totnes Church, Devon. Pat Russell

67 Baptistry panel for Stoneleigh Church, Warwick by School of Embroidery, Birmingham College of Art and Design. The inscription at the base is embroidered in satin stitch in thread drawn from the original fabric, over cardboard templates

When designing words, it must be decided whether the words need to be easily readable, as in banners or heraldry, or whether their legibility is of only secondary importance. The designer may be more interested in making an intriguing and satisfactory pattern, where the lettering content can be deciphered rather than read, than in making a direct statement in words.

66
67
68
69

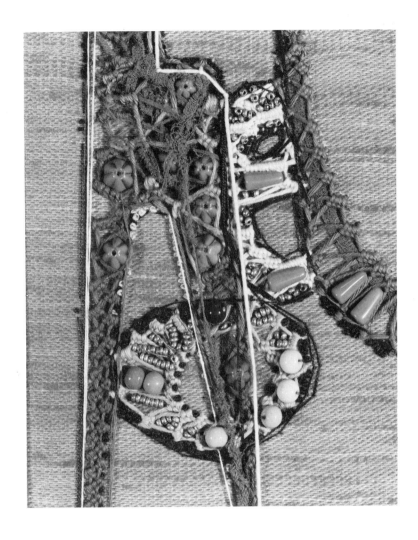

68a Embroidered design for Christmas card. Diana Springall

68b Original sketch showing arrangement of letters NOEL to form abstract pattern

69 Cope with Greek inscription. Pat Russell

49

In the first case where legibility is the first consideration, the letters should be evenly spaced, with no two letters appearing to be closer to each other than any other pair, the aim being to achieve a smooth rhythmic balance throughout the word. Note the use of the word 'appearing' above. This appearance of even spacing cannot be achieved by the use of a ruler, it must always be judged by eye. The eye when well trained is quite the most efficient measuring instrument available where visual aspects are concerned. As the eye can recognise a letter in all its numerous forms, so can the trained eye judge and assess the space required between the letters to produce a satisfying rhythm.

70 Detail from hanging. Pat Russell and Elizabeth Ward

There are, however, some general rules for guidance. For even spacing, the spaces in between each pair of letters will measure much the same in area. They will also relate to the spaces inside the letters themselves.

Thus the rectangular space between a pair of letters such as H and I, while bearing some relationship to the space inside the H, will be much the same size as the spaces between such pairs as H and A, A and V, H and O, and O and C. It will be seen that these areas can be worked out fairly easily.

More difficulties arise when considering the spacing of letters such as P and A, E and S and other pairs of more complicated letters. It is here that reliance must be put on the eye as a measuring instrument and the areas assessed visually. Even more necessary is the measuring power of the eye when it comes to the spacing of shaded letters (ie letters with thick and thin strokes)—for example the space needed between two thick strokes such as I and D will be subtly different from the space needed between a thin and a thick as in N and I (the eye will tend to 'jump' the thin stroke and take in some of the area inside the N when estimating inter-letter spaces) and the comparative spaces between A and V and V and A need very careful judgment. The notorious word in this category is BALACLAVA a formidable exercise!

71   To sum it up it can be said that two curved letters, eg OO or OC, are placed closest together, because the eye takes in the wider area between the tops and bottoms of the letters; a curved and a straight letter as HO or IG a little further apart; the widest gap of all being between letters with two thick vertical strokes as HI, IB, etc.

In the second case, where letter forms are used as the basis of a design but the main consideration is to produce a satisfying abstract composition, the question of spacing is more complicated and a much more personal problem. The rhythm need no longer have an even beat, but may be 'syncopated' and varied, perhaps to suit the purpose of the design or perhaps developed from a natural rhythm arising from the arrangement of the letters within that particular word or words. No rules here! The design potentialities of letters in a given word (or words) must be explored, analysed and developed, the final pattern being allowed to come from the inherent characteristics of the letters themselves and from the requirements of the design, and not superimposed by preconceived ideas. The qualities of proportion, balance, rhythm must always be kept in mind.

72

73

74

72 *Capricorn* wall hanging, 1800 mm × 1200 mm (6 ft × 4 ft). Pat Russell. The lettering was first designed in freely cut paper shapes arranged to relate to the other elements in the design. Note the dates in Roman numerals

◀

73 Lettering from Greek manuscript. Bodleian Library, Oxford

◀

74 Pulpit fall. Bodø Cathedral, Norway. Ester Tybring Struve

53

Designs may be developed from the use of letters with no reference to their context, the letters merely being used as motifs to be selected and assembled to form a satisfying whole. This can be fascinating and a prolific source of ideas but is not this perhaps avoiding the issue? A letter is surely only a letter because that particular arrangement of lines and curves has a specific meaning and is meant to be read. It is this problem of having to use given symbols in a certain order for a definite purpose, and the discipline that this involves, that is both the challenge and the fascination of lettering.

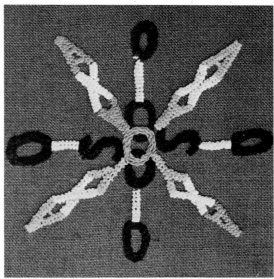  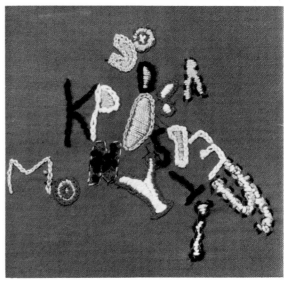

76a

76b

75

75 Abstract composition originating from letter forms. Student at Manchester Polytechnic, School of Embroidery

76a and 76b Design from random letter forms by 14 and 15 year old pupils at Churchdown Secondary School, Downham, Kent

Some most exciting abstract designs can however, be derived from using letter forms
only as a starting point and with no intention of retaining readable letters. As the design
develops, the actual form of the letter becomes unimportant and the design is allowed to
develop spontaneously from its springboard of letter forms. The designer selects and
develops only those parts of the letters, or of the spaces in between that interest him and
allows the composition to grow intuitively and freely. The result can be original and
satisfying, retaining only a half hidden reference to its basis of lettering.

75
76
77

77 Altar frontal by Charlotte Cope. Design based
on letters P A X

78

6 Arrangement of words

The problem of the arrangement of words in a design varies so much with each individual requirement that it is difficult to give any general rules for guidance; except to insist that if the words form part of a design involving other elements, they must be considered as an integral part of the whole composition right from the start and not be fitted in as some sort of afterthought in any space that happens to be left over. The wording must be so organised as to take its place happily with the other units and to harmonise with the general feeling of the composition. However one or two general hints may be given:

SPACES BETWEEN WORDS

When there are several words in a line, the spaces between the words should be kept to a minimum. This ensures that the rhythm of the line of lettering is interrupted as little as possible. If too large a space is left the design will look 'bitty' and the words will not read smoothly. Where several lines of wording are involved, the words should be so arranged that the spaces do not come underneath each other, as this will result in ugly vertical breaks or, in larger areas of texts, in vertical 'rivers' of space appearing. As a rough guide, the space between the words should be about the same, or a little less than the width of an O.

SPACES BETWEEN LINES

The spacing between lines of lettering can vary greatly, depending on the amount of wording to be fitted in and the result required. If a mass effect is wanted, the lines should be kept close together, or, for an all-over decorative effect, even touching. A larger space between the lines will give the effect of bands of pattern. It should be noted that, in general, a better design results if the spaces between the lines are greater than the spaces between words.

When organising the distribution of wording in a design, the sense of the wording must be kept in mind and if possible the words so arranged that the phrases fall naturally into place and read easily. If a symmetrical layout is chosen, lines consisting of one short

78 *Facing page* Detail from Sicilian quilt, depicting the story of Tristram, fourteenth century. Quilted in brown-red on unbleached linen. Crown copyright. Reproduced by courtesy of the Trustees of the Victoria and Albert Museum

word, such as *a, the, in,* etc. should be avoided as this weakens the composition. Words placed centrally must have their position adjusted by eye to 'look' central, eg a word starting with a straight sided letter, say H, and ending with an L will tend to appear to be slightly to the left of centre because of the open nature of the last letter and must be adjusted accordingly. Similarly, if say a straight margin is required on the left hand side, straight sided letters will be placed up against this margin, but rounded or diagonal strokes or open letters will have to be placed very slightly over the margin to make them *appear* directly under the letter above.

In formal lettering when using capitals only, the letters in each word should be all of the same size. An uneven effect results if for the sake of emphasis the first letters of important words are made larger. A similar unhappy 'sprinkling' effect is the result in a piece of lettering with contrasting coloured, or decorated, initial letters. Emphasis is best obtained by the use of larger or heavier letters, or of a contrasting colour, for the whole of the important word or phrase.

79 *Facing page* Panel, IN OMNES TE AMO. Anthea Nicholson, Goldsmiths College of Art, London

80 Detail from altar frontal, Pershore Abbey. Free machine-embroidered letters on organdie. Pat Russell

81 Sampler with verse from *On the nativity of Christ* by William Dunbar. Pat Russell

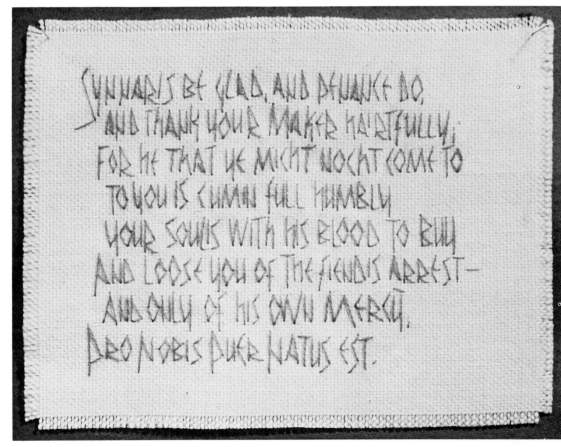

82 Detail from German table-cover. Sixteenth century. Crown copyright. Reproduced by courtesy of the Trustees of the Victoria and Albert Museum

60

7 Influence of tools, materials and environment

Apart from a purely abstract consideration of the design and layout of letters, the craftsman must also recognise the subtle influence exerted by the tools and materials which he uses.

As with the Roman letter the finely curved serif and the slightly concave form of the straight strokes arose directly from the free and expert use of the chisel on stone, so, in pen lettering, the letter forms are directly related to the movement of the square cut pen, held at a constant angle. The varying pressure of the engravers tool produced the characteristics and allowed the intricacies of copper plate writing and lettering drawn directly with a brush retains a free flowing quality.

Gerard Manley Hopkins

84   Pen lettering for title page of manuscript
book. Pat Russell

The embroiderer, in his approach to letter design, should always keep in mind his
own particular tools and materials.

Letter forms arising naturally from the honest and direct use of the tool with the
appropriate material will always have a 'rightness' and a unity of feeling in the quality of
their design. Most unhappy are the results where tools and materials have been abused
and made to perform feats alien to their character.

85   Engraved plate showing the formation of the
letter **S**, from *Magnum in Parvo; or The Pen's Perfection*
by Edward Cocker, London 1672. Crown copyright.
Reproduced by courtesy of the Trustees of the Victoria
and Albert Museum, London

86 Detail from frontal. Letterform arising from direct use of a pair of scissors

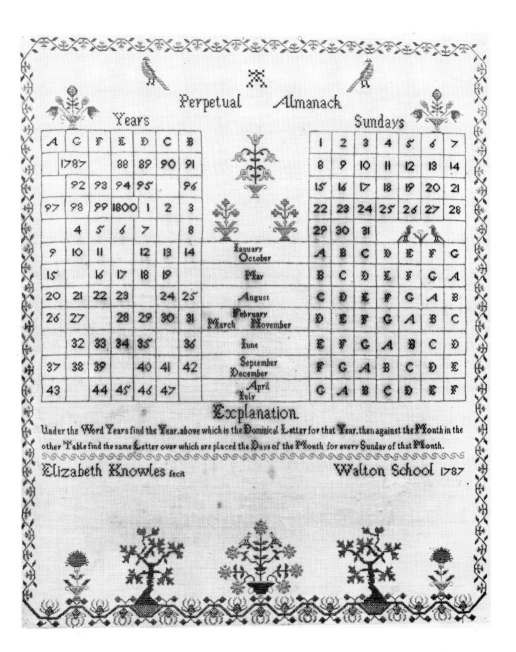

87 Perpetual Almanack worked by Elizabeth Knowles in 1787. Crown copyright. Reproduced by courtesy of the Trustees of the Victoria and Albert Museum, London

88 The Shepherd's Buss. Sixteenth century.
Crown copyright. Reproduced by courtesy
of the Trustees of the Victoria and Albert
Museum, London
Words in the verse have been replaced by
pictures
   The CUP of care and sorrow's CROSS
   Do clipse my STAR and SUN
   My ROSE is blsted (blasted) and my
   BONES
Lo DEATH inters in URN
   False CUPID with misfortunes WHEEL
   Hath wounded HAND and HEART
   Who SIREN like did LURE me
   With LUTE and charmed HARP

64

Children's alphabet panel. About 1200 mm × 610 mm
(4 ft × 2 ft). Pat Russell

Detail from ends of stole embroidered throughout with the words TAKE MY YOKE UPON YOU AND LEARN OF ME. Pat Russell

The consideration of letter design cannot be complete without giving thought to the environment in which the letter is to be seen and the function which it is expected to perform. These facts again will influence the letter form in many ways. Lettering on a banner will need to be formal and easily legible from a distance, the lettering on the notice on the door of a child's room can be light-hearted and gay, while fancy can be allowed its fling where a decorative effect is the major consideration.

The best and most satisfactory lettering is that in which the possibilities of the tool used to form it, the qualities of the material used to make it, the nature of the environment and the purpose for which it is planned have all been considered and exploited to their full.

89 Frontal for Norman chapel of St Edburgha, Pershore Abbey. Pat Russell. For detail see 182 page 128

90   Door inscription for a boy who keeps budgerigars.
Pat Russell

91 The Hereford cushion. Late sixteenth century.
Crown copyright. Reproduced by courtesy of the
Trustees of the Victoria and Albert Museum, London

92a   Detail of stole depicting Jonah from the tomb of
St Cuthbert, Durham Cathedral. Reproduced by permission of the Dean and Chapter of Durham Cathedral

92b   Detail of maniple depicting the Deacon Peter.
Also from the tomb of St Cuthbert, Durham Cathedral.
Reproduced by permission of the Dean and Chapter of
Durham Cathedral

8   Lettering and embroidery

The techniques used in embroidered lettering fall into two main categories: appliqué work and stitchery.

The best known examples of lettering in early embroideries all come into the second category. The Bayeux Tapestry, made in the eleventh century to record the Norman conquest of England, gives the story in picture form and also incorporates the narrative in Latin. The wording is in simple single stroke letters with straight serifs and is carried out in stem stitch. In the stole and maniple of St Cuthbert in Durham Cathedral the names of the saints are embroidered in a heavier type of letter and the names fit happily into the

93   The death of King Edward. Section of the Bayeaux Tapestry

94 Full view of Sicilian quilt depicting the story of Tristram. Fourteenth century. For detail see 78
page 56. Crown copyright. Reproduced by courtesy of the Trustees of the Victoria and Albert
Museum, London

95 *Facing page* Oxburgh hanging,
Marian, circa 1570. Green velvet
with an all-over interlaced pattern
worked in couched cord with red
silk and gold thread. 37 panels are
applied, of various shapes and sizes.
Mainly worked in cross and tent
stitches. Crown copyright. Reproduced by courtesy of the Trustees of
the Victoria and Albert Museum,
London

70

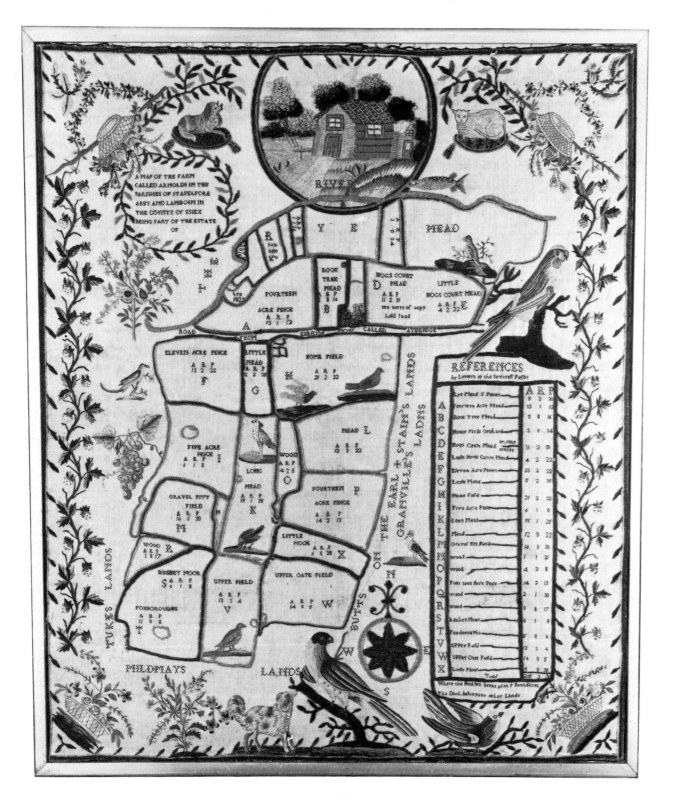

96 Sampler map. Late eighteenth century. Crown copyright. Reproduced by courtesy of the Trustees of the Victoria and Albert Museum, London

97 Machine embroidery and cut net techniques. Pat Russell

98 Banner *Priestly Benediction* in the collection of the artist, Joan H. Koslan Schwartz. Appliqué (reverse and direct) metal threads and surface stitchery ▶

99 Sketch for wall hanging by Constance Howard for the Northampton Museum. It depicts the history of shoe-making through the ages ▶

areas around the figures. The story of Tristram is the subject of a fine narrative embroidery on the Sicilian Quilt in the Victoria and Albert Museum. Made in the fourteenth century, the figures and the lettering are carried out in quilting on natural linen in brown thread. Lettering is also to be found in the Oxburgh hangings made by Mary Stuart and the Countess of Shrewsbury in the sixteenth century, much of it in the form of monograms. The vogue for working samplers in the seventeenth to nineteenth centuries produced a spate of lettering in cross stitch of various forms. Few samplers are produced in this less leisurely age; however the present trend of using letters and lettering in decorative forms and in design may renew interest in this subject and initiate a revival, though possibly in less time-consuming form.

Appliqué work is one of the oldest forms of embroidery and it is difficult to understand why no early examples of lettering in this technique are to be found. For today's embroiderer, with the enormous variety of fabrics available and with the advent of the electric sewing machine, it is a field of endless potential. It is a particularly suitable technique for lettering, giving scope for free and direct methods of working. The wide range of fabrics encourages adventure in colour and texture and a boldness in approach to design, while the electric sewing machine certainly allows for speed of execution.

100 Banner for St Luke's Church, Barrow-in-Furness. Pat Russell. The lettering sits happily in the space below the bull and forms an integral part of the design

9 Appliqué lettering: choice of letter form

Letters should be appropriate in shape and character to the tools and materials used in making them, and to the purpose for which they are intended. The overall character of the lettering must be the first consideration. This will depend on the general intention of the composition and the purpose for which the lettering is included. Is its main purpose to be informative and therefore easily read? Is it one feature in a complex design, of parallel importance with other motifs? Or subsidiary to other motifs? Or is the lettering to form the basis of a complete design in itself? Do we wish it to be legible or merely decipherable? Or maybe the aim is an abstract composition, where the basic structure of the lettering is hidden in a pattern of colour and shapes? Perhaps, if one is left with an exciting abstract design it does not matter if the original letter form disappears. All these considerations, and many others, will influence the choice of letter form. Whatever the aim may be, the design of the lettering must be appropriate and carefully worked out with the final purpose of the composition always kept in mind.

Other major factors to be considered are the tools and materials at the disposal of the embroiderer.

In appliqué lettering, the materials are fabrics of all types: the tools, a pair of scissors and a sewing machine, or needle, and thread. The letters are to be cut out: therefore their character should be appropriate to the action of the cutting instrument, a pair of scissors. Their shape will tend to be angular and any curves will be restrained, for niggly or tight curves would not come naturally to the free cutting movement of a good pair of scissors. Scissors are the tool automatically associated with cutting fabrics but where a very firm, non-stretchy fabric is to be used, a sharp craft knife may serve better. The resultant shapes will be similar to those cut with scissors but more complex curves can be cut out in this way. In some cases the application of adhesive interlining to a fabric before cutting out will prevent fraying and allow for more accuracy in cutting. Care should be taken that the adhesive interlining does not have a detrimental effect on the appearance of the fabric involved. This method is particularly useful in cutting smaller size letters.

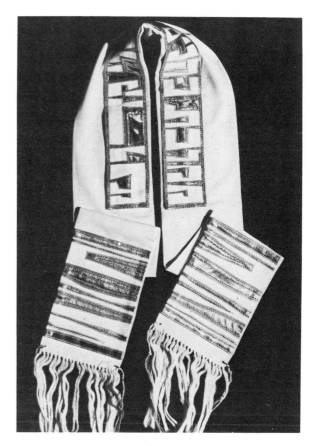

101 Hebrew lettering on prayer shawl: 'A nation of priests and holy people'. Gold appliqué and couched gold threads on wool crepe. Pat Russell

75

102 Embroidered and screen printed panel. Pat Clarke, third year student, Manchester College of Art and Design 1969. The design was derived from an original basis of lettering but was allowed to develop into a completely abstract composition.

The letters are to be sewn down by hand or by machine. The choice of method will depend on the qualities of the fabric and on the effect required. Some fabrics stretch badly or 'move' when machine sewn, therefore hand sewing may be a necessity, if accuracy is to be maintained. On the other hand, in a freer type of design, it may be more interesting to exploit this stretchy quality and to allow a more varied letter form to develop. If an accurate and precise letter form is required, the fabric and method of sewing down must be chosen accordingly. Conversely, given a particular fabric, the form of letter most suited to the qualities of that fabric must be selected.

The size of the lettering is also a factor in determining the materials and methods to be used. It would not be feasible, for instance, to machine down very small letters. Letter forms, fabrics and methods of sewing are, therefore, interdependent and success will only result in the happy correlation of all three.

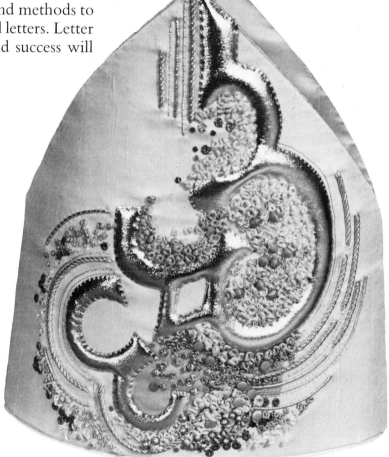

103   Mitre by Andree Mendham, third year student, Manchester College of Art and Design 1969. The design was developed from an idea derived from a carved misericord reminiscent of the symbols **A** and Ω. The letter forms themselves are almost obliterated in the final design

104 Alphabet book, page size 254 mm×
267 mm (10 in.× 10½ in.). Pat Russell and
Pru Russell

105 Set of cushions in cherry red corduroy,
the letters in white corded silk, sewn down
with several rows of straight machine stitching and a final edging of machine satin stitch.
Pat Russell and Jane Dorman

106 Lettered super-frontal for St Michael's Chapel, Pershore Abbey. Pat Russell. The lettering which reads LORD EVERMORE GIVE US THIS BREAD is transformed into a band of abstract pattern by the tonal arrangement of the appliquéd fabrics

ABCD	Futura Medium
ABCD	Futura Bold
ABCDEF	Univers 67
ABCD	Futura Display
ABCD	Optima
ABC	Albertus
ABC	Dartmouth Roman
ABC	Clarendon Bold
ABC	Cooper Black
abcdefg	Futura Display
abcde	Clarendon Bold
abcde	Cooper Black

10   Appliqué: designing the lettering

For the more formal work, letters adapted from the Roman will be found to be most suitable. These can be based on suitable type faces, some of which are illustrated here. Sample alphabets can be found at the end of the book. If space is not available for these classically proportioned letters, which tend to be wide in proportion to their height, a more condensed version of the letter may be used. This may also have the effect of giving more weight and prominence to the lettering. Emphasis may also be given by increasing the thickness of the letter strokes, but this must not be taken to extremes in formal lettering. 107

Lower case letters may also be used but the design impact of these is sometimes weakened by the fact that the ascenders and descenders (the parts of the letters above and below the line) may detract from the bold 'band of pattern' characteristic of the lettering. If it is used, it is desirable to keep the ascenders and descenders as short as possible. 107

In the context of modern embroidery techniques these formal traditional letters can seem out of place and lacking in vitality. A freer letter form may be found to be more in keeping with contemporary work. This may be evolved from the traditional letters by the cut paper method. Each letter is cut out freely in paper, the shape and proportion being basically that of the traditional letter but with the natural variation arising from use of scissors or knife being allowed and exploited. The 'family relationships' of the letters discussed in the first part of the book are respected and maintained but the character of the letter is transformed from a somewhat mechanical shape to something showing the direct influence of the hand and tool, a lively and personal variation on the theme of the original letter. The amount of variation will depend on the general character and purpose of the design and on the personal choice of the designer. 108
109
112

Another form of free lettering can be designed by building up the letter forms from strips of paper of varying width. The disposition of thick and thin strokes need not necessarily correspond to the disposition of the thicks and thins in traditional letters. Their placing can be entirely governed by the design considerations of the wording involved. This technique can be used also with lower case letters. 110
111

113

108 Directly-cut paper letter, based freely on traditional letter form *cf* Albertus type face opposite

109 Directly-cut paper lettering showing heavier form of letters

110 Part of design for orphrey of cope. Condensed form of letter built up from strips of paper

111 Lettering built up freely from strips of paper. Note the importance of the spaces in-between

112 Directly-cut paper design showing condensed letter form. See 90 page 66

113 Lower case letters built up from strips of paper. Note the short ascender of letter **d**

Facing page

107 Type faces. Capitals suitable for appliqué work. Only the heavier and more condensed type of lower case letter is suitable for appliqué work

Other designs may be arrived at by using traditional letters in an informal way.

Designing lettering is at the start a long and rather laborious process depending very much, until experience is gained, on a process of trial and error. But the hard work is essential and unavoidable. All the real creative effort goes into the design at this stage, and the success or failure of the whole project depends on the quality of this initial work.

Designs for lettering should, if possible, be drawn or pasted up full size. When a large design is in hand, it will probably be found more convenient first to make a fairly accurate scale drawing of the design on squared paper and to enlarge this up. Drawn letters must be filled in with colour or shading, especially in the early stages of the design so that the shapes inside and between the letters can be accurately assessed as units of the design. In enlarging, the small scale original must not be adhered to absolutely rigidly—the large scale letters may need some adjustment when seen full size. Cut paper letters are best designed initially full size, the letters being freely and directly cut out and tried in position. The letters are cut and re-cut, and arranged and re-arranged until a final satisfactory layout is achieved. When using cut paper, do not attempt to draw the letters first. The letters

114 Felt hanging DOMINUS ILLUMINATIO MEA. Pat Russell. Design carried out in cut paper. The letters were then cut out of the felt background and materials of varying colours and textures placed underneath to show through. They were secured by a line of straight machine stitching through the felt close to the edge of the letters

115 Felt letter collage. Pat Russell. The letters cut out from a dark-coloured version of the above were rearranged to form a completely different design

take very little time to cut out and rejects can be discarded and fresh letters cut in far less time than it would take to draw them, and the result will have a freshness and spontaneity impossible to achieve by laborious pencil work. Remember all the time to observe and assess the value of *the spaces in between*. An effort of the imagination and a few tryouts will soon help to decide on the size and type of letters required.

If the overall design calls for the lettering to stand out in sharp contrast to the background, work the letters in white paper or newsprint on a black ground or vice-versa. If less contrast is required, use newsprint and brown, or black and brown paper. The use of newsprint can be a great help, as the width of the lines of print will help in cutting the letters all to a similar size.

In all lettering designs, remember the importance of retaining a 'family characteristic' throughout the alphabet: treat the curves in the B P R C G, etc. in the same way as you treat the O, and let the straight parts of all the letters bear a family resemblance to each other.

As the letters are cut out, pin them into position, watching carefully the shapes that are forming between and inside the letters. As the design develops, watch and assess the value of the spaces between the words and between the lines.

If the lettering is one of a number of design elements in the work, check continually against the rest of the design to ensure that the weight and character of the lettering harmonises with the whole. If the work is large and will normally be viewed from a distance, stand back frequently and review the work from as far away as possible; if available, use

116 Conventional letters used unconventionally. These designs were evolved using transfer letters (*Letraset*). If the letters are arranged on squared paper, the task of enlargement becomes much easier. Enlarging can also be achieved by a projector, if this is available

117 First sketch on squared paper for Mothers' Union banner. Pat Russell. The detailed designing of the letters was carried out full size

a reducing glass. When it is felt that a satisfying arrangement has been achieved, it is advisable to leave the work for a few days. It can then be reviewed with a fresh and critical eye and any necessary alterations can be made. Do not be satisfied until it is felt that the design is 'just right'. Patience and persistence are required at this stage but the result will be well worth the time and effort expended.

When the design can be taken no further, paste the letters down firmly and accurately in position and the 'master design' is ready.

Another method of designing lettering suitable for appliqué work is to make small experimental arrangements of the letter forms using a wide pen or a brush. The most successful of these sketches is then developed and refined until a satisfactory design is achieved. The final design is then made by enlarging this to the required size. The use of a *Grant* enlarger or projector if available considerably facilitates this process. If an enlarger is not available, it would be best to do the initial work on squared paper.

118   Station of the Cross III. Pat Russell. Experimental design made with wide pen

119   Above design enlarged to full size. The letter forms are sharpened and refined

120   The completed embroidery

11   Appliqué: Lettering into embroidery
Transferring and sewing down

In coming to the problem of interpreting the 'master design' in terms of embroidery, the treatment and method chosen will again depend on the over-all effect required and on the end-purpose of the work. Whatever is decided, the aim should be to make the lettering look 'at ease' with the other elements of the design and form an integral part of the whole composition. On the practical side, the aim is to sew letters on to their background efficiently in an appropriate and workmanlike manner. Where the lettering fits naturally into a separate panel or section, eg as in the orphreys of a cope or the border of a banner, the area of lettering can be worked separately and be mounted into position afterwards.

121   Whitsun frontal for St Mark's Chapel, Alban-Neve Centre for the Deaf, Luton. Pat Russell and Elizabeth Ward. The lettering and its background are worked separately and later sewn into position

If it is decided that the lettering should be all in the same fabric and colour, a simple method of working is as follows:

Take the background material and the material to be used for the letters and tack them together, right sides upwards, making sure that the lettering area is well covered by the lettering material. The lines of tacking must be close enough together to ensure that the materials do not shift. Make an accurate tracing of the lettering from the master design. (A roll of greaseproof paper is cheap and efficient to use for this purpose.) Tack this down firmly, face upwards on top of the other materials, being careful to get the placing of the design accurate. The lines of tacking should go vertically across the lettering as well as at the top and bottom. Carefully and accurately machine round the outline of each letter, using a straight stitch and with the top machine thread matching the lettering material. On most materials it is advisable to follow this with two or three further rows

122 Diagram showing stages of transferring letters to fabric by machining through tracing, letter material and background fabric, tearing away tracing paper and cutting away surplus letter fabric. The letters would need further embellishment to hide obvious holding stitching

of straight stitching slightly inside the first one. This will counteract any tendency for the material to pull away or to fray at the edges. It can also be treated as a decorative feature. Care should be taken, however, that the stitching is accurate and does not blur the edges of the letters, thus losing the crispness of the design. The tracing paper is then torn away and the top material carefully cut away from around each letter. The letters can then be finished with a line of machine zigzag stitching, on top of the straight stitching.

123   An alternative method would be for the design to be transferred to the background fabric by pricking and pouncing or by the use of a tracing wheel and dressmaker's tracing paper. Each letter would then be traced and cut out separately, pinned and tacked into position. This method might not be suitable for very frayable materials although the doubtful material could, if suitable, first be backed with adhesive interlining. The separate letter method has the advantage that any adjustments necessary, perhaps arising from the character of the fabric used, can easily be carried out and it is also useful to the more experienced designer who may prefer to allow the design to develop with more freedom. It also can be used where the colour of the letters needs to be varied. Methods of sewing down would again be variable. Zigzag machine stitch, strengthened by one or several rows of straight stitch, invisible hand-sewing or a decorative stitch would all have their place.

123 Design transferred by dressmakers' tracing paper and wheel to fabric. Letters cut out separately and placed in position

A further method would be for the letters to be traced on to thin card or thick paper,
cut out and each letter covered in the desired fabric, the fabric being turned in at the edges
and fixed with adhesive to the underneath of the card. If required, padding could be used
on the upper side of the card to give a raised effect to the letter. The letters would then be
placed in their positions, already traced on to the background, and sewn with invisible
hemming stitches.

124 Showing the letter cut in card, padded and half-
covered with fabric. The final letter has been finished
with two strands of couched Japan gold

12 Appliqué: Lettering into embroidery Embellishment

After this initial sewing down of the letters is completed, the work should be looked at and examined with a critical eye. Decide whether the letters are positioned exactly in their right places and if necessary, make alterations. It is difficult to alter basic letter design and spacing after this stage and essential adjustments made now will be found to be well worth the effort.

Next, decide whether the letters 'stand' in their present form in relation to the whole composition, or whether some extra treatment or embellishment is needed. If the letters have an appearance of completeness and look 'happy' in their context, no more need be done to them. But if they still look like 'cut fabric letters sewn down', their integration with the rest of the design is incomplete and further work will need to be done to them.

A simple and straightforward method, and therefore often a successful method, of embellishment is to outline the letters in some way. This has the advantage of disguising the stitching used for sewing them down which sometimes may appear obtrusive. It will also help to ensure that the letters are well and truly affixed to their background. This outlining can take many forms. It may be done with couched thread, wool or braid; in matching or contrasting colours or in gold or silver, or it may be worked in decorative hand stitchery. It may also be done by machine, using zigzag or straight stitch, or a combination of both. Wools, threads and braids may also be applied by machine, either by straight stitching through the centre of the strand (some wools stretch badly under the machine) or by zigzagging over the top. Here interesting effects can be obtained by using contrasting colours.

Care must be taken that the outlining is not clumsy and out of proportion to the size of the letter. Watch also that the letters do not get distorted or 'out of true' in the process. Conversely the outlining can sometimes be very useful in correcting any small irregularities in the letter forms that may have crept in during the sewing down. Large faults or irregularities, it must be noted, can only be corrected by unpicking and resewing.

125

127

128

125 Letter edged with buttonhole stitch in two colours to give three dimensional effect

126 Burse. Dorothy Kavanagh, second year student, Manchester Polytechnic School of Embroidery

90

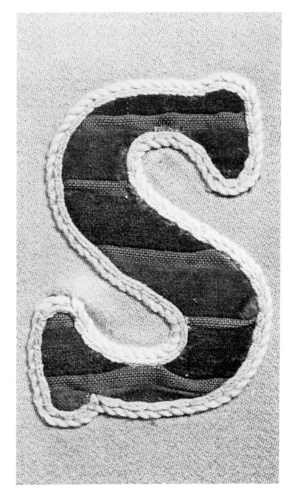

For further decoration, the face of the letter may also be enriched by hand em-
129 broidery or by machine stitching, or by a combination of both. 'Scribbling' or texturing
with machine stitching is very effective in the right context. Colours and textures can
130 be enhanced by a simple hand stitching or by more lavish hand embroidery.

What form this embellishment takes is the choice of the embroiderer and it will depend
much on her skill and sensibility.

As a general rule, and especially in formal embroideries, it is best to use 'over-
embroidery' with restraint and only when for some reason the work calls out for added
emphasis of this sort. In most appliqué lettering, a careful and imaginative choice of
fabrics, with an eye to their colour and textural contrasts should provide sufficient lively
variation. Nevertheless, in skilled hands this aspect of the work can be most exciting.

127 Letter **N** edged with several rows of straight
machine stitching and an outline of wool, sewn
down with machine straight stitching through the
centre of the strand

128 Letter edged with couched thread and cord

129 *Facing page* Detail from altar frontal. Appliqué letters, based on stencil letters, enriched with hand embroidery. Jane Dorman, School of Embroidery, Birmingham College of Art and Design

130a Stole end embellished with machine stitching and simple hand embroidery. Pat Russell

130b A chalice veil. The finials of the cross consist of the letters Alpha and Omega, with a border inscription in English and Bulgarian. Worked as gift from the Archbishop of Canterbury to the Bulgarian Patriarch. 760 mm (30 in.) square. Machine embroidery techniques. Pat Russell

131 Detail from Festival Frontal, Alban-Neve Centre for the Deaf, Luton. The gold kid letters need no embellishment. The background has been enriched with layers of black net and organdie, chain stitch and straight stitch machine embroidery

132 Lettering built up from pieces of fabric and embellished with machine stitching

133 Detail from Lent frontal, Alban-Neve Centre for the Deaf, Luton. Here the black felt letters stand in sufficient contrast to the varied colours and textures of the background fabrics, themselves enriched in places with couched threads and machine stitching

134 Detail TOWARDS MEN from orphrey of cope. Pat Russell

13 Appliqué: Lettering into embroidery Pressing and mounting

When the work is completed, it should be inspected carefully to see that all ends are securely finished off, tacking threads removed, etc. It should then be stretched, pressed and mounted.

Pressing may be done from the back with an iron, or the work may be stretched over a damp pad and left to dry. If an iron is used, care must be taken not to overpress. The character and vitality of some fabrics can be destroyed by too much heat, pressure or steam. If gold or silver leather is used, keep the iron well away from it. Sometimes, particularly with machine stitchery, the work will be found to have contracted considerably in the process of embroidery. This can usually be rectified by careful stretching before pressing. Place the work face downwards on a soft board (such as insulating board) which has been covered with a pad and ironing sheet. Working round the edge, from the centre of each side and end, gently pull out the embroidery and stab-pin it through to the board, 135 at 35 to 50 mm ($1\frac{1}{2}$ in. to 2 in.) intervals keeping the material 'square'. This process is repeated until the work is stretched to the required size. Sometimes it is not possible to regain the original dimensions exactly and when starting an embroidery, this fact should be anticipated and adequate allowance made to allow for this possible shrinkage. When stretched as far as possible, the work is pressed with a steam iron or with a damp cloth, the amount of pressure used depending on the thickness and type of material involved. Allow to dry, remove the pins and turn face upwards.

If an iron is not used the work is similarly stretched but over a damp pad and with the right side of the embroidery upwards. It must be allowed plenty of time to absorb the damp and to dry.

When the work is in the form of a banner or hanging, it is then interlined with calico, dowlass or other suitable material, and lined and mounted as required. If planned as a rigid panel, a piece of board or wooden frame of the required size is prepared by covering it with calico tacked into place. Mark the centres of the top, bottom and sides of the work 136 and of the frame. Place the embroidery over the frame, matching key marks; stretch

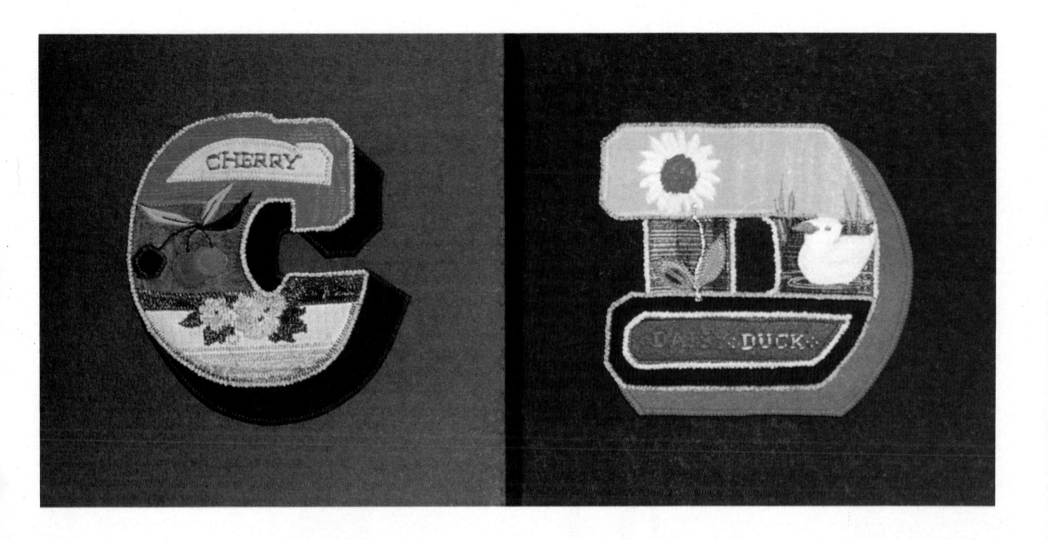

Pages from embroidered alphabet book
Pat Russell and Pru Russell

Festival frontal for St Mark's Chapel, Alban-Neve
Centre for the Deaf, Luton
Pat Russell and Elizabeth Ward

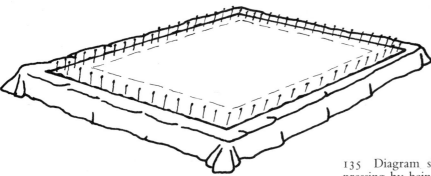

135 Diagram showing work being stretched for pressing by being pinned out on a covered padded board: face downwards if it is to be pressed with a steam iron: face upwards over a damp pad if an iron is not to be used

136 Diagram showing finished work being stretched on frame. When taut and square the frame is turned over and the final tacks put into the back of the frame. The side tacks are then removed

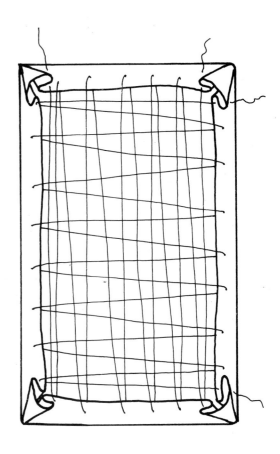

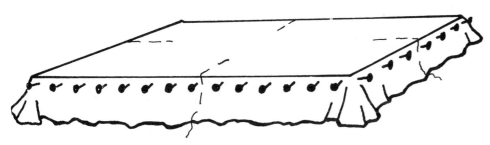

gently and tack lightly to the *edge* of the frame at about 50 mm (2 in.) intervals. Do not drive the tacks fully home. Check that the work is central and square and that no creases or wrinkles have appeared. Make any corrections by removing tacks where necessary and gently pulling and adjusting until all creases are eliminated. Turn the work over and tack to the *back* of the frame, keeping the material taut and driving the tacks firmly home. Finally remove the tacks from the edges of the frame.

Smaller pieces of work can be stretched on a board or strong card by criss-crossing the back with strong threads and drawing these up gently until the work is taut and all creases disappear.

137 Work stretched by criss-cross threads at the back of the board or frame

138 This fifteenth century German embroidery shows lettering well integrated with other design units. The letter forms in the top border are Gothic lower case letters. The letter on the scrolls are based on the Lombardic capitals, usually found in manuscripts of the period in association with Gothic writing. Crown copyright. Reproduced by courtesy of the Trustees of the Victoria and Albert Museum, London

14 Stitchery: Lettering into embroidery
In-filling by hand

In the context of stitchery, embroidered lettering may again be considered in two main categories; one, lettering in which stitchery is used to fill in the whole area of the letter and two, lettering in which the shape and character of the letters is determined, or very directly influenced by, the type of embroidery stitch employed.

Designs for lettering for work in the first category will be worked out very much in the same way as those for appliqué lettering. Instead of the design being built up from the interplay of the colour and texture contrasts of fabrics, the infinite variations obtainable from the use of embroidery stitches are used. Stitches may be used to fill in both letter and background or else the letter form or background may be covered with stitchery.

138 For example, in tapestry work, the whole area is filled in with stitchery, the letters being defined by a change of colour or, more subtly, by a change of texture in the stitches. In
139 Assisi work, only the background is worked, leaving the letters to appear in the basic fabric.

139 Italian Assissi work showing background filled in with stitchery and letter-forms left blank. Crown copyright. Reproduced by courtesy of the Trustees of the Victoria and Albert Museum, London

140 Canvas work exercise, using letter forms by Margaret Kerston, aged fifteen, Churchdown Secondary School, Downham, Kent

141 Detail of panel from Oxburgh Hanging *Marian*. The monogram MARY STVART, flanked by two thistles surmounted by a Royal Crown and flanked by two more monograms. Around the border, not easily distinguishable SA VERTU MATIRE, an anagram of MARY STVART. Crown copyright. Reproduced by courtesy of the Trustees of the Victoria and Albert Museum, London

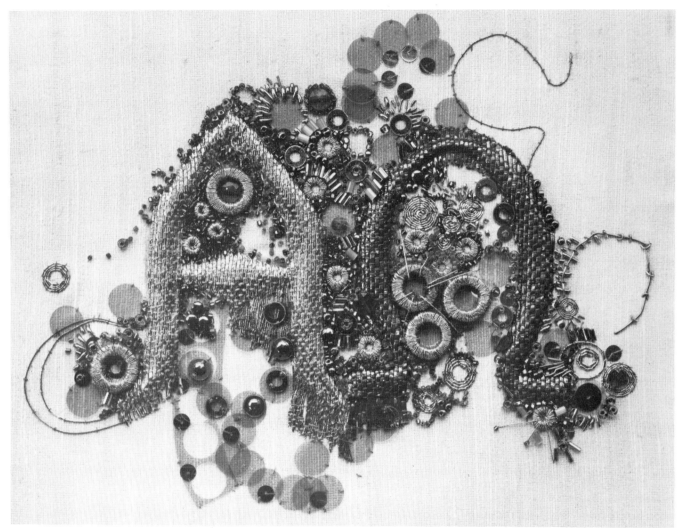

The same design considerations discussed in the chapter on appliqué lettering apply when designing for embroidered lettering of this sort. The form of the letters must reflect the particular qualities of the tools, materials and methods used and, as always, environment and fitness for purpose must be considered an important factor of design. A very wide range of letter forms is open to the embroiderer in these designs, as it can probably

142 Burse, using Alpha and Omega. Student at Manchester College of Art and Design. Embroidery carried out in acetate, gold thread, sequins and beads, and silk fabric

be said that a stitch can be found or invented to fill any situation. However the most successful work will result from an imaginative and sensitive choice of embroidery stitch in relation to letter form or, of course, of letter form to stitch.

The character of the letter and the character of the stitchery must unite to make a happy marriage in the context in which they are brought together, and each must be right for the other in scale and in quality.

Letter forms may also be adapted from the Roman or any other type faces and both capitals and lower case letters will be found suitable.

Free lettering, based on cut paper designs or on brush or pen lettering, can be used most successfully. Letters with fine lines or with fine serifs which would be unsuitable for appliqué work can be used for this technique subject to the choice of an appropriate embroidery stitch.

143
144

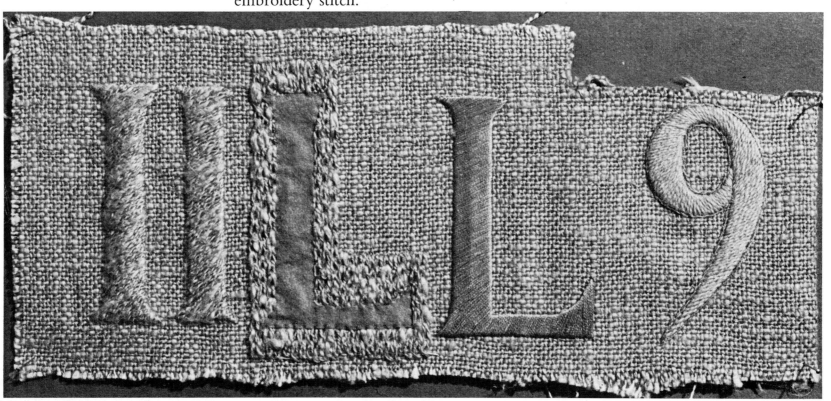

143 *Facing page* Early experiments for Roman lettering used for Baptistry Panel, Stoneleigh Church, Warwick by School of Embroidery, Birmingham College of Art and Design
(a) Worked in slanting satin stitch in a thread drawn from the background fabric over a padding of straight lines of Anchor soft laid up the vertical (b) The same stitch worked over a thin card template (c) The letter was cut in felt and surrounded by lines of chain stitch worked very closely in a thread from the material. (a), (b) and (c) depended for their effectiveness on the slub character of the withdrawn thread (d) A contrasting smooth treatment using stranded cotton over a card template (e) Two ply wool used for slanting satin stitch, outlined in stem stitch in stranded cotton. Version (a) was finally used for the inscription EVELYN HILL 1883–1966 MORS JANUA VITAE at the base of the panel. See 67 page 48

144 White-work based on traditional letter form with thick and thin strokes and serifs, adapted to suit embroidery stitch used. First Dell'Addolorata G. L. Righetto, Milan

While it is probable that a suitable stitch can be found for almost any letter shape, it must be appreciated that the character of some embroidery stitches will exert a subtle influence on the shape of the letter. For instance, if it is proposed to use a 'fill-in' stitch based on counted thread work fine curves would be difficult to produce accurately. Thus letters with elegant curved serifs would not be appropriate. The bolder curves of the letters themselves however, while not being reproduced exactly would take on an interesting characteristic of their own. For any stitch that has a definite geometric structure, it is advisable to use squared paper when evolving the design, especially where the letters concerned are small in relation to the size of stitches. If, however, the letter is large and the stitchery small, this would not be so essential, nor would it be where it was proposed to define the letters with an edging of some sort.

148

The choice of stitchery open to the embroiderer is almost endless. Satin stitch in its many forms is adaptable and the obvious choice for smaller letters: long and short stitch, laid work in all its various forms, cross stitch, rows of chain stitch, french knots, irregular sprinkling of small stitches (seeding), couching, fly stitch, feather stitch: the skilled embroiderer has many stitchery techniques at her command. They can be used singly or in combination with each other in endless permutations: size of stitch can be varied, and thickness of thread, and each can be combined with the excitement of colour contrast and harmony. Their infinite variety is limited only by the skill and imagination of the embroiderer.

145   Letter **P**. Kathleen Norris. Circles made from coiled felt around a glass bead arranged round a flat button and down the stem of the letter, interspersed with square glass beads spiked with bugles and joined together with cable chain stitch. Blues and purple on blue ground   *cf* 32 letter **P** page 27

146   Letter **P**. Cynthia Kendzior. Couched metal braids and lurex cords. Applied gilded snakeskin

147   Child's embroidered initial. Churchdown Secondary School, Downham, Kent

148   English sixteenth century chalice cover. The letters are based on contemporary lettering, their distinctive decorative form arising from the counted thread technique of the embroidery. Crown copyright. Reproduced by courtesy of the Trustees of the Victoria and Albert Museum, London

150 Burse ST LUKE. Susan Gaskell, first year student, Goldsmiths College of Art. Dark olive green furnishing fabric, couched gold passing and crinkle thread, large and small pearl purl, with padded circle in different gold purls forming a cross

Overleaf

151 The letters on the following pages were taken from a complete alphabet worked by Kathleen Norris on 26 squares of furnishing fabric, each square a different colour. They were intended to give a fresh look to familiar patterns which fitted into a given space. They are worked in gay colours with as varied threads as possible, using very simple stitches rather than set techniques in academic forms.

S Free needle weaving on placed threads on the surface to imitate string constructions. These threads all enter the material in one spot at the top or at the bottom and are then whipped or darned to form patterns. Cream on turquoise ground

Q Flat appliqué of heavy silk outlined with chenille and silk threads. These textures are so rich that no extra interest is needed, but a few rosette chain stitches have been worked in the spaces to prevent too severe an effect. Purple and black on blue.

A Straight lines of couching with variation in yarns. Coloured pearls added for gaity and to break the stiffness. Pinks and mauves with a touch of yellow on a light brick red ground.

M Letter in white kid from which a pattern has been cut out to show the padding underneath, a red jersey cloth with lurex thread. The beads are Victorian cut steel. Red, white and silver on grey ground.

F Massed french knots worked in blocks and outlined with simple straight stitches. Frequent colour changes give movement. Cream, turquoise, olive green and light brown on yellow ground.

I Circles squares and rectangles were buttonholed and filled with various cut work fillings and then attached one by one to pink and orange satins. The surface stitches are a type of chain stitch also in pinks and orange. On a cream ground.

N Black organdie appliqué with bold stitchery, composite and knotted stitch and spider wheels. Emerald, purple, yellow, and pink on dark grey.

G Long and short stitch overworked with bullion knots and twisted yarns to add textural interest. Pinks, reds, greens and a little white on yellow ochre ground.

Z Letter in glass tesserae on plastic cloth, secured with strands of thick cotton thread, threaded through beads. Multicoloured on dark blue ground.

L An attempt at continuous line treatment with couched silk and beads edging a shot silk appliqué. The horizontals in the stem become vertical at the base and so catch the light in different ways. Crystal, grey, mother of pearl on grey.

R Rich mosaic-like texture built up of small pieces of bronze kid, copper plate and beads on a cream ground.

Y Straight stitches in rayon floss round blocks of raised chain arranged around a stem of thick couched threads, stem thickened at base with raised chain stitch. Many changes of colour three to four to each block getting progressively darker, from white through yellows, lime, to deep orange. Blue ground.

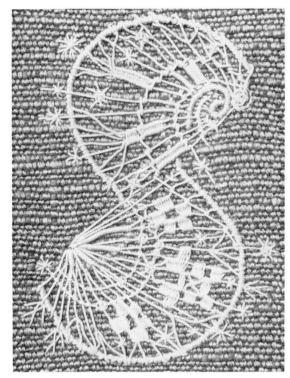
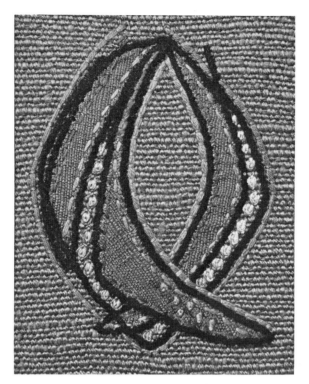
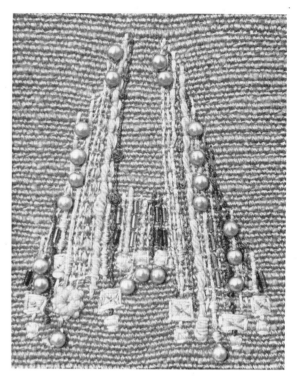

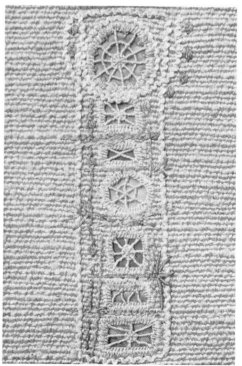

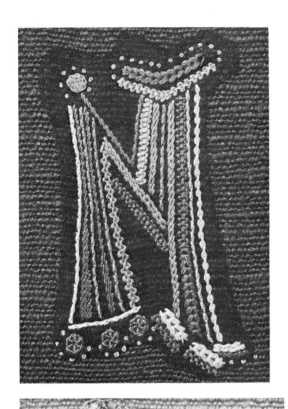

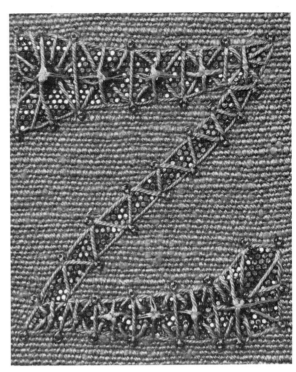

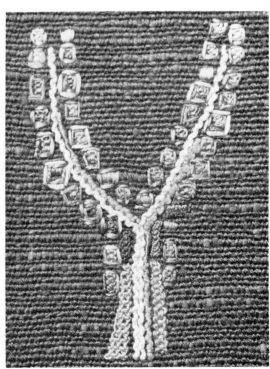

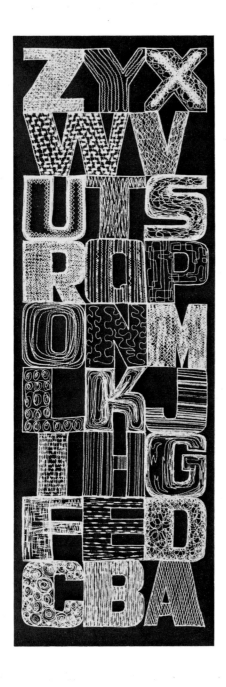

15 Stitchery: Lettering into embroidery
In-filling by machine

This in-filling of the letters may, of course, also be carried out in machine embroidery. It may take many forms, from random 'scribbling' in straight or zigzag stitch to geometrically accurate patterning with automatic machine embroidery stitches. A session of experimenting will soon demonstrate the diversity of pattern and texture that can be achieved in this way.

In many cases this concentration of machine stitchery will tend to make the work pucker or will distort the fabric. If there is any danger of this, the fabric must before working, be stretched on a machine embroidery frame. This unfortunately can sometimes inhibit freedom of design especially with large letter forms as only a limited area can be worked in the frame at one time and it is necessary to stop work frequently to change its position. On some fabrics, it may be possible to produce a satisfactory result by backing the fabric with a firmer material or by the use of vanishing muslin. For free machine embroidery, the use of a frame is essential except in very skilled hands. Here the presser foot is removed and an embroidery foot inserted. The feed teeth are lowered and the stitching is directed by moving the fabric by hand in varying directions, backwards and forwards, side to side, and round and round, producing a great variety of all over free patterning and texturing. In every case the nature of the patterning must in some way relate to the shape and size of the letter and to the character and feeling of the whole composition.

152   Alphabet panel in machine embroidery white thread on black felt. Pat Russell

153 Details of machine stitches

Z Cross hatching with straight stitching

Y Free embroidery, simple zigzag following structure of Y

X Free machine embroidery with interweaving lines concentrated in centre of letter strokes

W In-filling of vertical and horizontal lines consisting of small straight stitches alternating with zigzag stitching, same stitch length

V Free embroidery following figure of eight movement

U Letter outlined with zigzag stitching of graded stitch length, constant width

T Backwards and forwards stitching in zigzag vertical movement, long stitch length

S Free embroidery with zigzag stitch, the lines of stitching echoing the shape of the letter and concentrated towards the edges

154 R Zigzag stitching of constant width
      sewn horizontallly and vertically
   Q Letter filled in with vertical lines of
      zigzag stitching of varied stitch
      length and stitch width
   P Free embroidery with line changing
      direction each time through ap-
      proximately 90°
   O Free embroidery with lines of
      stitching following circular motion,
      echoing shape of letter
   N Free embroidery meandering line
   M In-filling of zigzagging in vertical
      direction, with random concen-
      tration of stitches
   L Free embroidery with circular
      motion
   K Free embroidery straight stitching
      following shape of letter
   J Letter filled in with horizontal lines
      of zigzag stitching of various widths
      and lengths of stitch

155 I Horizontal lines of zigzag alternating with straight stitching with vertical free embroidery straight stitching superimposed

H Letter filled in with vertical lines of straight stitching of varying stitch length

G Backwards and forwards straight stitching freely following shape of letter, stitching concentrated towards edges

F Backwards and forwards straight stitching in vertical and horizontal directions

E Horizontal lines of small straight stitches thickened at intervals by backward and forward stitching

D Free embroidery entanglement, concentrating towards the edges

C Free embroidery in spiral movement

B Vertical lines of stitching swelling from straight stitch to full width of zigzag and back again. Each line was then over-stitched with a line of straight stitching

A Lattice pattern of straight stitching

156 Detail of panel. Lettering partially filled in with net appliqué and backwards and forwards machine stitching. If the letters are of an appreciable size, or if the work in which they are to be incorporated is large and cumbersome, the letters may be worked individually and mounted in position when complete

157 Free version of nineteenth century decorative letter outlined with two layers of machine satin stitch, the first layer being slightly narrower and acting as padding for the second. Jane Dorman

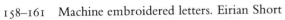
158–161 Machine embroidered letters. Eirian Short

158 T Appliqué net letter with free embroidery on
Irish Machine and some hand embroidery
159 S Shadow appliqué with whip stitch decoration. See page 131 for details of whip stitch
160 C Free machine embroidery
161 H Free embroidery on domestic machine

162 Unfinished panel. The background around each letter is textured with free machine embroidery 'scribbling'. The embroidery is carried out on black net and superimposed on grey and brown tweed. Both top and bottom threads of differing colours are used in the machine embroidery. Pat Russell

163 *Facing page* Eighteenth century sampler. Note the disconcerting use of capitals and lower case letters. Crown copyright. Reproduced by courtesy of the Trustees of the Victoria and Albert Museum, London

16 Stitchery: Lettering into embroidery
Letter forms from hand embroidery

In the second category of lettering in the context of stitchery are to be found all those letters whose form arises from or is directly influenced by the type of embroidery stitch employed. The most obvious and familiar examples of this are to be found in the numerous samplers worked mostly during the last two centuries. Many of these include alphabets, both upper and lower case and pertinent inscriptions and quotations, the whole embellished with charming decorative motifs and border patterns. In all cases the letter form arises directly from the geometric arrangement of the cross stitch which, because the scale of the letter is small compared to the size of the stitch, imparts a very distinctive character to the lettering. It is surprising how very legible most of these letters are. More surprising to the present day embroiderer is the number of hours which must have been spent pursuing this occupation! but it undoubtedly has a fascination all of its own.

A study of the subject matter of samplers may well be rewarding. Their scope is wider than at first appears and this aspect alone could provide a fund of inspiration to today's embroiderer seeking subjects for her craft. See figures 61 and 96. If the idea of carrying out an appreciable amount of lettering by this technique is daunting, the designer may turn to other ways of reproducing lettering in terms of stitchery. An alphabet can be evolved using a minimum number of straight lines for each letter which is eminently suitable for carrying out in that simplest of stitches, the straight stitch. Bearing in mind the principles of letter design discussed earlier in this book, a number of interesting alphabets in both capitals and lower case can be produced. The simple and direct nature of their construction gives them an attractive unity of design and they should not be found to be too time-consuming or laborious. Their counted thread structure naturally imparts a certain rigidity of design. A more free approach abandoning this geometric basic can result in lively and very personal interpretations and might well be a field for exploration. See third line of Sampler, figure 169, and figures 168 and 81.

169

164

165

166

Mary Wakeling Ended This December The Tenth 1742 Aged Ten Years

164 Nineteenth century sampler showing family record. Crown copyright. Reproduced by courtesy of the Trustees of the Victoria and Albert Museum, London

165 Eighteenth century sampler showing highly ornate alphabet exploiting to the full the decorative quality of the type of stitches used. Crown copyright. Reproduced by courtesy of the Trustees of the Victoria and Albert Museum, London

166 Napkin and napkin ring for Susan. Edna Henderson. The repeated letter S forms the border pattern of the napkin and a more complex arrangement of the S form decorates the napkin ring

167 Eighteenth century sampler. Crown copyright. Reproduced by courtesy of the Trustees of the Victoria and Albert Museum, London

168 A robin red-breast in a cage. Free straight stroke lettering similar to line 3 of sampler

169 Sample alphabets from simple straight stroke letter forms. Pat Russell

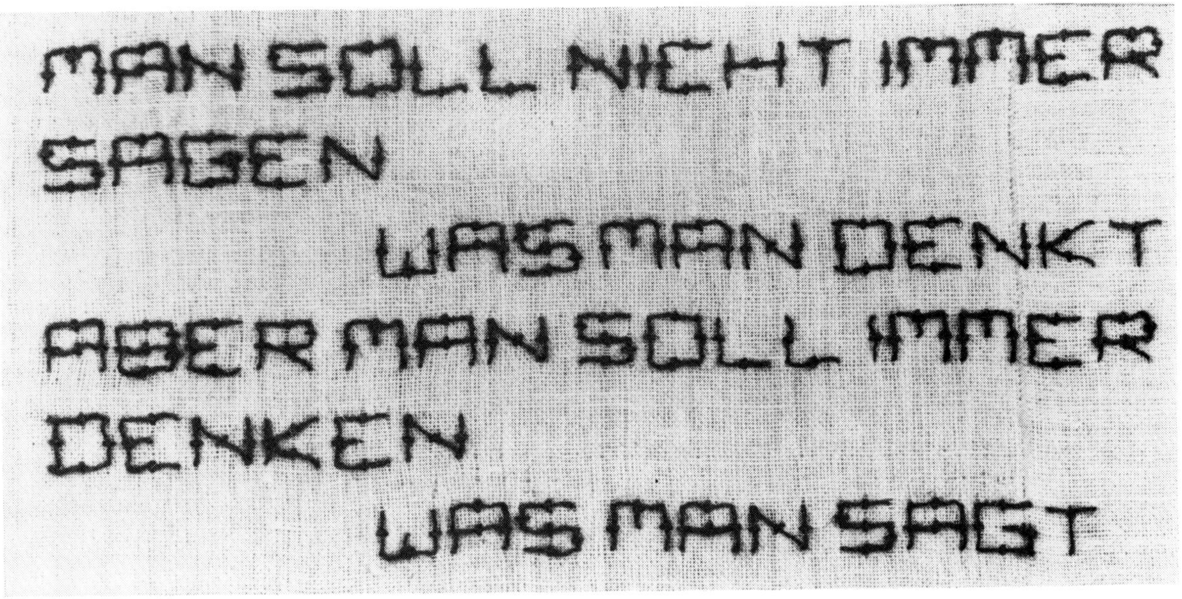

MAN SOLL NICHT IMMER
SAGEN
            WAS MAN DENKT
ABER MAN SOLL IMMER
DENKEN
            WAS MAN SAGT

170 Simple letter forms making good use of the decorative possibilities of the technique of couching. Student teacher, Basle, Switzerland

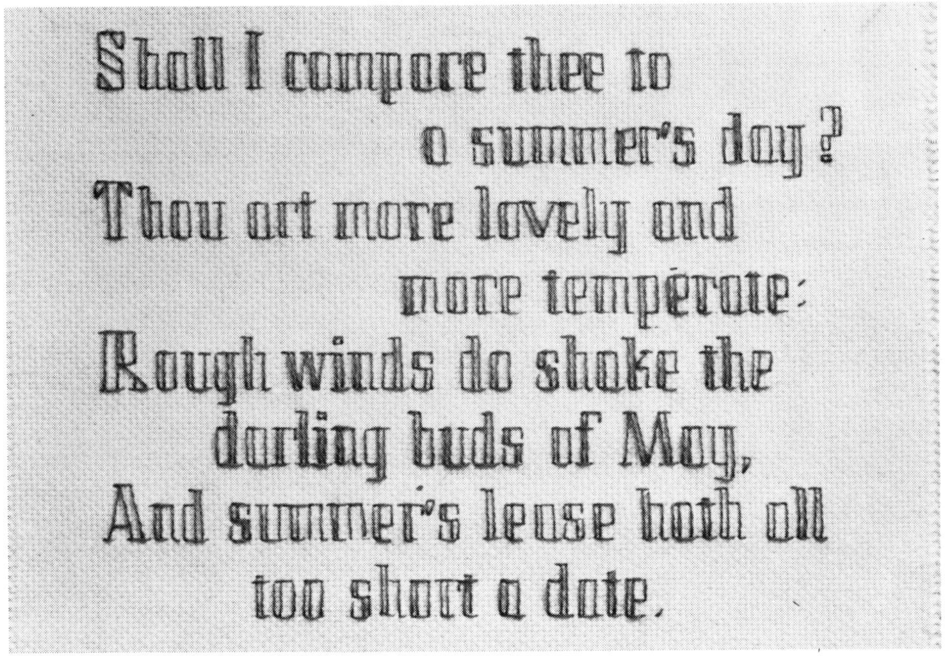

Shall I compare thee to
            a summer's day?
Thou art more lovely and
            more temperate:
Rough winds do shake the
            darling buds of May,
And summer's lease hath all
            too short a date.

171 Sampler. Pat Russell. At first sight this lettering appears conventional. Upon closer examination, it will be noticed that each letter has only one thick vertical stroke instead of the usual two *cf* line 12 of sampler in 168 page 120

Other embroidery stitches will no doubt suggest other letter forms or modifications. Where small amounts of lettering are concerned, their variety is unlimited. Embroiderers might like to sign their work with their own distinctive mark. Stitches such as stem stitch or chain stitch may be used to outline or delineate letters, without influencing their design to any great extent; or several different types of stitches may be combined; lines of stitching may sometimes be extended to build up the entire face of the letter. The cursive nature of chain stitch makes it very suitable for reproducing handwritten words, signatures or cursive lettering of any sort. Couching of all sorts, or the use of braid or ribbon would likewise be suited to this sort of lettering. The technique of quilting can also be used for lettering. See figure 172 a – e.

172a

172c

172b

172a–e Initialled squares from a 'Friendship Quilt' made towards the end of the nineteenth century

172d

172e

173 Name on a handkerchief. Nineteenth century.
Reproduced by courtesy of the Embroiderers' Guild,
London

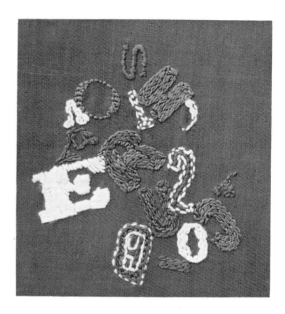

175 Child's embroidery exercise using letter forms. Churchdown Secondary School, Downham, Kent

174 Centrepiece for nursery tablecloth. P. Miller

177 Chinese symbol for longevity adapted by Cynthia Kendzior from stone carving, Kedleston Hall, Derbyshire. The thick and thin yarn used has an affinity with Chinese brush writing

176 Valentine embroidered in *Sylko*. Pru Russell

179 Wallhanging *Pennant Race*. Joan H. Koslan Schwartz. Surface stitchery on cotton

178 Panel. Mary Kirwan, third year diploma student, Goldsmith School of Art. Emerald green silk background embroidered in scarlet and orange red wools and stranded cotton

181a

181b

180 Unfinished canvas embroidery. Valerie Yorston, third year diploma student, Goldsmiths School of Art, London. In yellows, greenish yellows, cream and brown wools and cottons

181 Spectacle case for R. P. H.   Edna Henderson
(a) Front
(b) Back. Note the all-over design constructed entirely from the letter H
(c) Line drawing of design 181 (b)

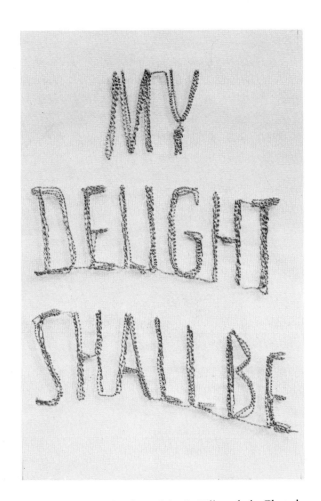

182 Lettering for frontal in St Edburgha's Chapel, Pershore Abbey. Pat Russell. See 89 page 65

Lettering worked directly by machine stitchery will have a character all of its own, the qualities peculiar to machine work producing lettering quite unlike that produced by hand.

For machined lettering, free embroidery techniques are probably most suitable, although machine stitching using the normal presser foot can also be used. 185 183

For free embroidery, the feed teeth are lowered (or covered with an embroidery plate) and a darning foot may be used. In both cases it is probably best to use an embroidery frame. This keeps the material taut and flat, ensuring a clear view of the work as it progresses; it also prevents puckering.

Fabrics must be chosen to suit the type and size of letter and, of course, must be appropriate to the piece of work as a whole. A closely woven, firm material is generally preferable. If the lettering is to be incorporated in a large work, the lettering is worked separately and stitched into position when completed. Should an accurate guide be needed the letters are first drawn and transferred to the fabric in the usual way. Or the letters can be sketched in directly on to the fabric with a brush, using water colour of almost the same colour as the background. This ensures that the guide lines do not rub off in the process of working and will show up enough to be followed. They will not show through embroidery obtrusively afterwards.

Lightweight, simple letters may be formed from single lines of straight stitching; heavier lettering is obtained by widening the throw of the needle and using a very small stitch (machine satin stitch). More fanciful lettering will arise from the use of zigzag stitches of various widths and lengths and from the use of automatic machine embroidery stitches. A characteristic 'machine-cursive' look results if the thread is not finished off at the end of each letter and word but is allowed to carry over to the next letter.

Interesting and appropriate letters evolve from using a 'scribbling' motion which roughly follows the pattern of a conventional letter form. A useful and effective stitch for machine embroidered lettering is whip stitch. This is produced by tightening the tension 185

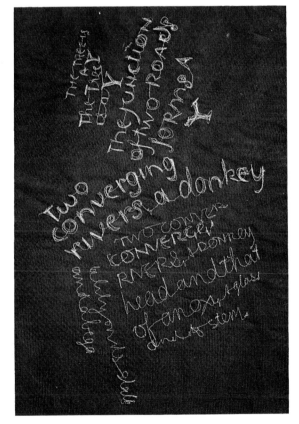

183 Experiments in machine embroidered lettering, using embroidery frame and normal presser foot

184 Machine cursive. Experiments in machine embroidered lettering, using embroidery frame, and free embroidery techniques

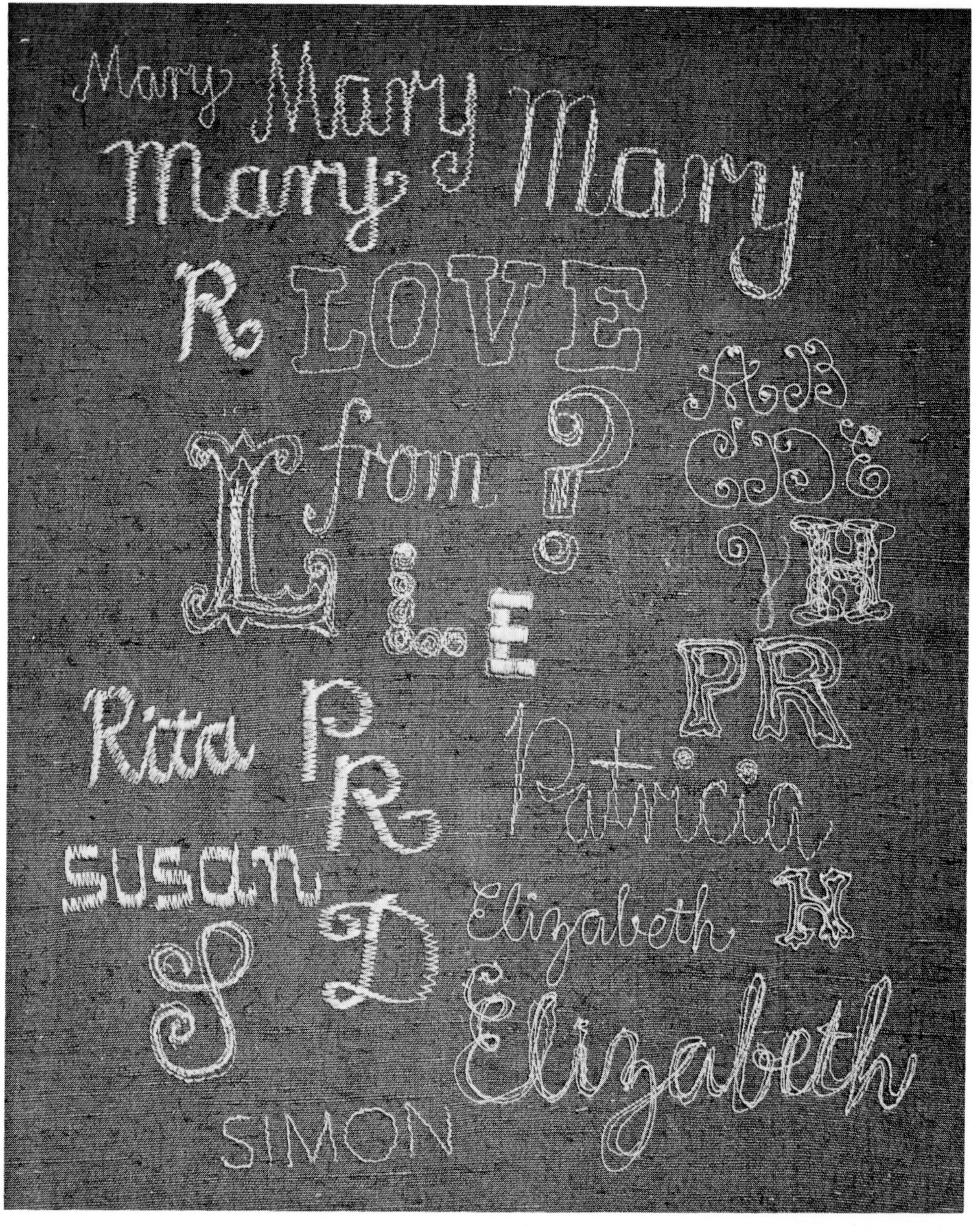

Mary Mary
Mary Mary
R LOVE
from ?
L i E
Rita P R
Patricia
PR
Susan
Elizabeth H
S D
Elizabeth
SIMON

of the top thread on the machine and loosening the spool tension until the thread runs freely. Using free embroidery techniques the fabric is moved slowly so that the lower thread whips over the top thread with small close stitches. The upper thread, which lies on the surface of the fabric, acts as padding for these stitches, producing a corded effect. Experiments can be made to test the effect of various combinations of tensions, weights of thread and speed of fabric movements.

Patient and accurate stitching can probably produce almost any form of letter, provided that the scale is not too small, but the most interesting lettering will be found to emerge from a freer use of machine techniques, allowing the particular qualities of machine stitching to influence the character of the letter.

Experiments will show the endless possibilities of lettering by machine embroidery; The designer's task is to select and to develop those which are most suitable to the project which he has in hand.

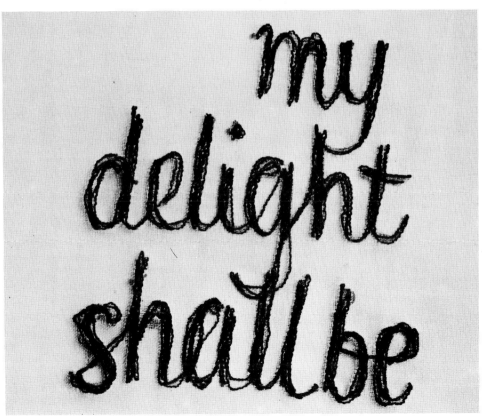

185 Experiments in free machine embroidered lettering using straight stitch, zigzag stitch and whip stitch

186 Free machine embroidered cursive lettering. An experiment for the lettering on the frontal for St Edburgha's Chapel, Pershore Abbey. See 89 page 65

187 Preliminary experiment for lettering for banner of Arms of Oxford University. The letters are freely based on the Roman letter form. They were first sketched onto the organdie background in white poster colour and then sewn using free embroidery techniques and a controlled 'scribbling' movement. Several versions were produced, the most satisfactory one being used for the final banner. The thread was allowed to carry over from one letter to the next

DOM MINA
INUS TIO
ILLU MEA

188   Banner. Pat Russell. Arms of Oxford University

Alphabets

The alphabets suitable for machine embroidery on pages 136, 137, 138 and 139 and the notes are taken from *Bernina Sewing Manual* Number 16 'Monograms', and are reproduced by kind permission of Bernina Sewing Machines.

These machine embroidered letters should be worked on an embroidery frame. A test piece should always be worked first, using the same material and thread as for the final work.

On starting, draw the lower thread up through the material inside the letter. Sew several plain stitches up to the starting point. Cut off both thread ends.

189 Experimental lettering. To obtain a quilted effect, the velvet background was backed with foam plastic. Using normal sewing foot and matching sylko, the letters were machined directly with little previous planning. A square form of letter was chosen. At the end of each letter was thread was finished off and pulled through to the back. Unfortunately the second line was started too high up and this makes the quotation difficult to read, nevertheless the general visual effect is pleasing and the technique would warrant further development. Size 300 mm × 300 mm (12 in. × 12 in.)

i   *Embroidered with straight-sided satin stitch*
Work with embroidery frame and foot
Satin stitch—set to required width
Needle position at centre
Do not forget the test-piece.

ii   *Work as i*
The wavy, horizontal parts of the letters E, F,
etc. can be sewn with the appropriate Bernina
fancy stitch, threading two upper threads
through the needle and lengthening the stitch
slightly.

iii *Hand guided embroidered letters*
Work with embroidery frame
Central needle position, without presser foot
Lower feed dog
Lower take-up lever (also without presser foot)
otherwise the upper-thread tensioner remains
open
It is best to thread lower thread in the bobbin
case through the spur (as for buttonholes)

If the feed dog is not used, ie the work is guided
by hand, ensure that only the frame is guided.
Any finger pressure on the material prevents
even flow and results in irregular stitching.
The continuous line marked should be in the
centre of the zigzag. Move frame as through
writing but do not twist. Let machine run fairly
quickly but guide frame slowly and steadily to
obtain even stitching.

iv   *Work as iii*
Turn hoop to sew horizontal lines. Observe
stitch position in horizontal of letter A.

v   *Work as i*
For all vertical and horizontal satin stitching.
When sewing sloping sides, however, first ensure
that the needle is set to the outer side of the stitch,
then embroider angle by enlarging the zigzag
from zero to the width of the satin stitch. At the
end of the sloping side, first change needle
position to the other side, then zigzag back to
zero to finish off the satin stitch horizontally.
Curves should be embroidered as in hand guided
lettering.

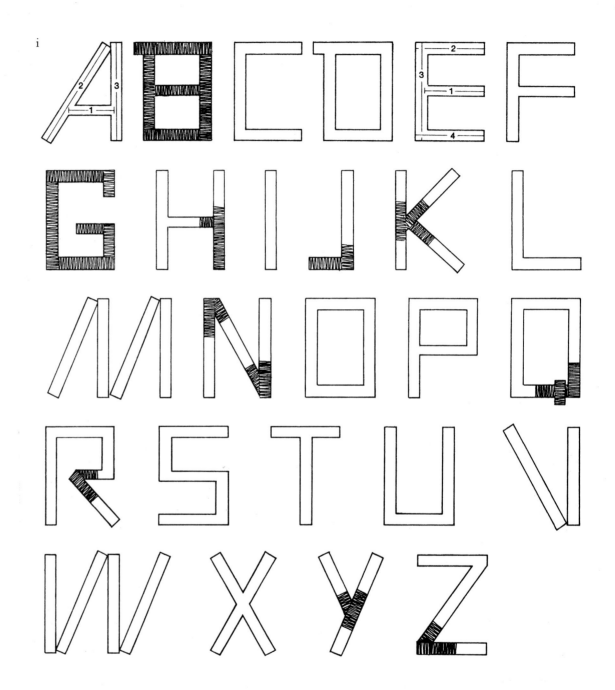

ii

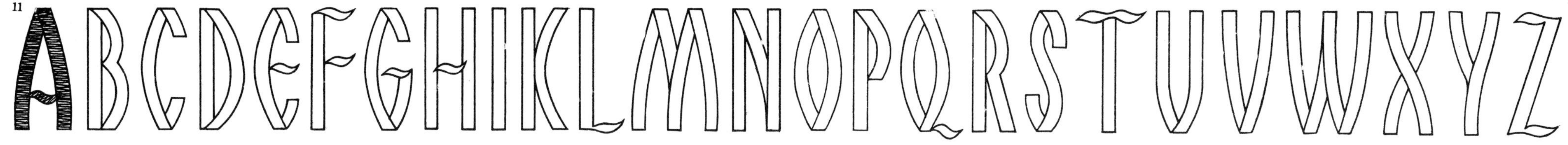

ABCDEFGHIKLMNOPQRSTUVWXYZ

iii

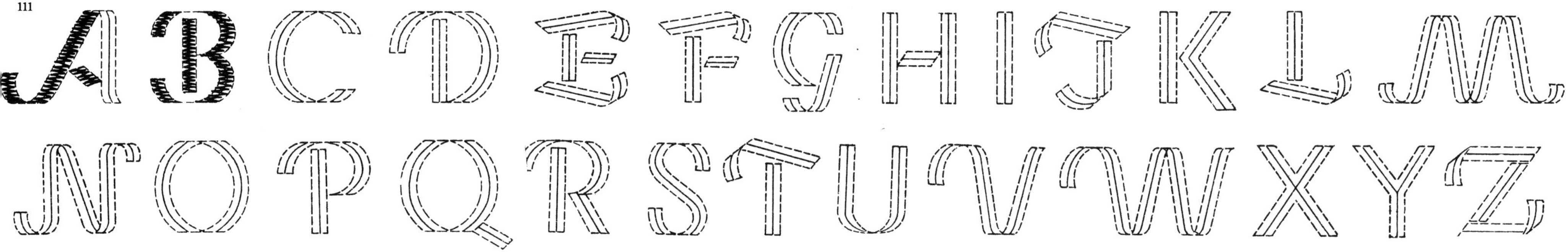

ABCDEFGHIJKLM
NOPQRSTUVWXYZ

iv

ABCDEFGHIKLMN
OPQRSTUVWXYZ
1234567890 0

v

ABCDEFGHIJKLMN
OPQRSTUVWXYZ
1234567890

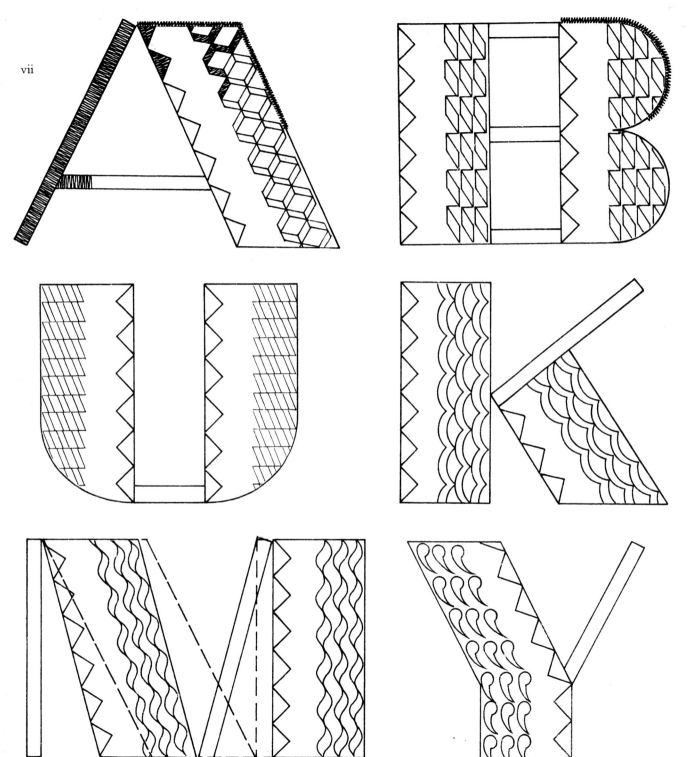

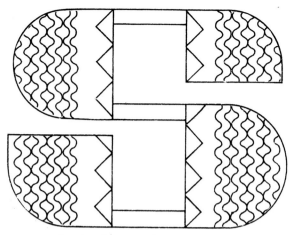

vi *Use embroidery frame and foot*
First embroider the fancy stitches using the indicator, then the satin stitch. The colours of the various fancy stitches can be varied as required

vii These large letters can be embroidered in the same way as vi but using more fancy stitches. The effect is even better if the wide surfaces are first appliquéd.

For appliqué lettering
Strengthen back of material with adhesive backing
Trace monogram *in reverse* on back
Baste appliqué material on material side
Use embroidery frame, particularly with soft materials
Sew the traced outline into wrong side of the work.
Zigzag $\frac{1}{2}$–1, stitch length $\frac{1}{4}$–$\frac{1}{2}$
Neatly cut off surplus appliqué material along the stitches
Turn over outline on right side. Zigzag $1\frac{1}{2}$—2 and satin stitch using thread in colour of appliqué material
After cutting back the material, the fancy stitching is done first followed by the turn-over sewing along the appliqué material and finally the strip pieces with a wide satin stitch. When sewing the fancy stitch pattern the fancy stitch indicator should be used. Thread 30 (Swiss 30/60)

Further details about sewing can be found in *My Bernina Guide*. Information on choice of thread, needle thickness, etc is contained in *Bernina Sewing Manual* Number 7.

139

190 A kneeler designed for the eleventh-century crypt of Worcester Cathedral. Lettering and decoration based on Romanesque illuminated manuscripts

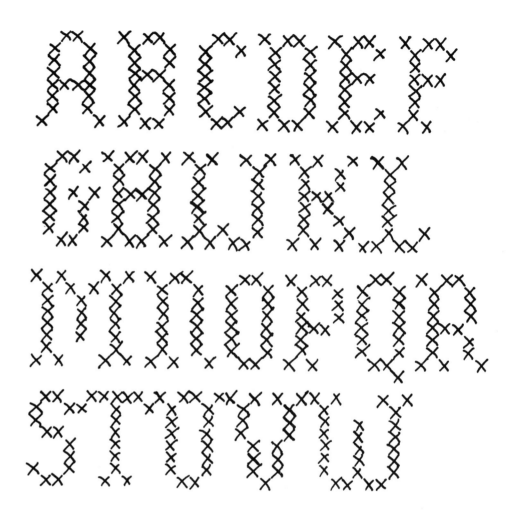

viii *Simple alphabets and numerals for samplers*

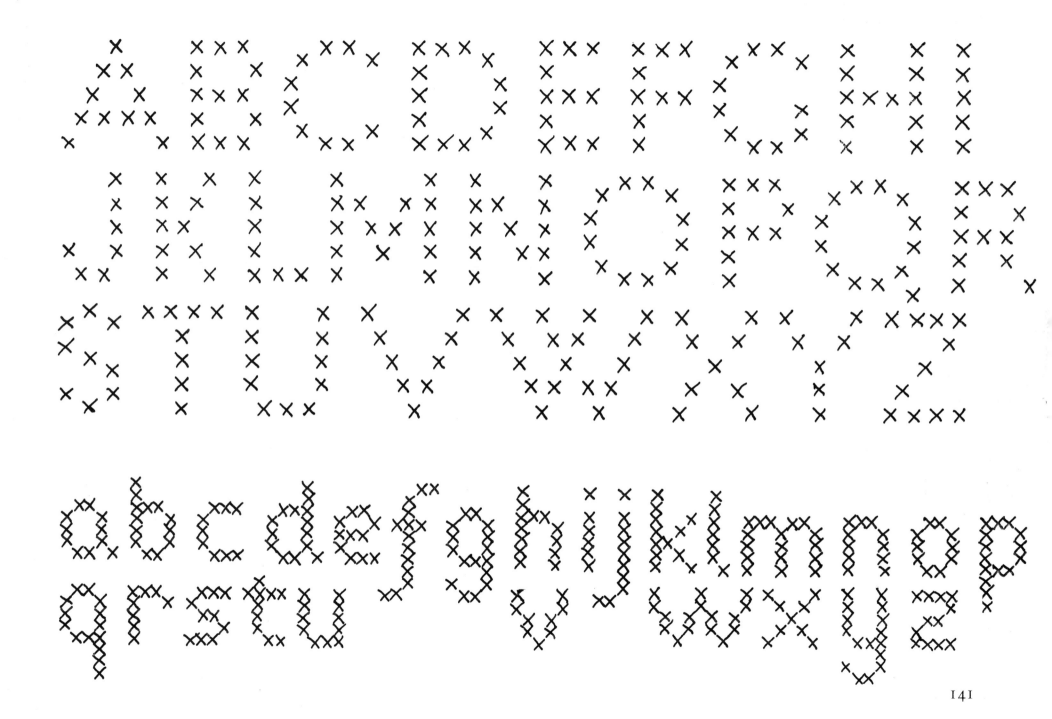

ABCDEFGHI
JKLMNOPQR
STUVWXYZ

abcdefghijklmnop
qrstuvwxyz

The alphabets on the following pages are examples of letter forms that may prove useful to the embroiderer. They are included rather to act as a starting point for letter designs than as patterns to be slavishly followed. Embroidery methods used and the personal preference of the craftsman will do much to determine their final form. They are printed on squared paper to facilitate enlargement or reduction by mechanical means. The squares will also act as a guide in keeping the proportions of the letters should they be freely copied by hand.

Many of the letters are from the *Letraset* range of transfer letters and a study of their extensive catalogue may be rewarding as a source of ideas. *Letraset* letters, most of which will not be large enough for embroidery purposes, may be transferred to graph paper and thence enlarged to the required size, or if available, a *Grant* projector may be used.

ix Alphabet adapted from the traditional Roman letter ▶

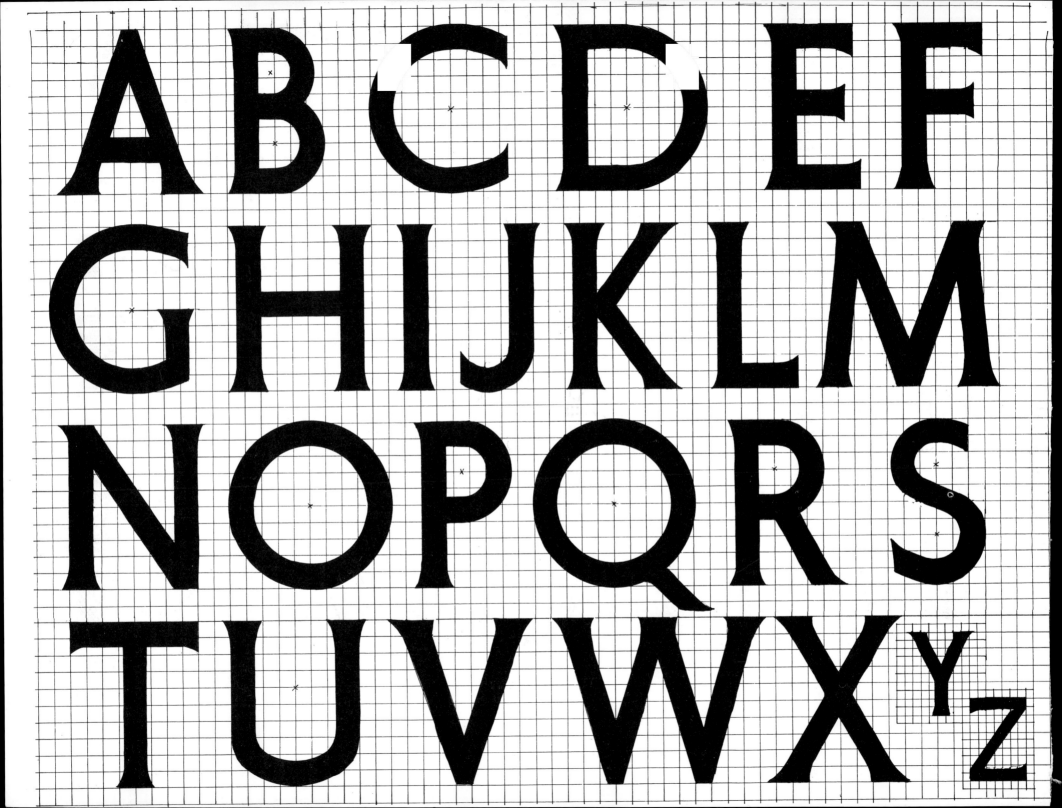

ABCDEFGHIJKLM
NOPQRSTUVWX
YZ

xi   Fry's Ornamented. A version of the traditional letter form which will suggest various decorative possibilities to the inventive embroiderer

STUVWXYZ

xii   Othello. A free adaptation of the block letter *cf* 108 page 81

ABCDEFGHIJKLMNOPQR

◀ x   Traditional block letter (ie letter with all strokes the same thickness) with the addition of a slight serif

xiii   Raffia initials. An intriguing letter of classical proportions, which obviously has a close affinity with embroidery

145

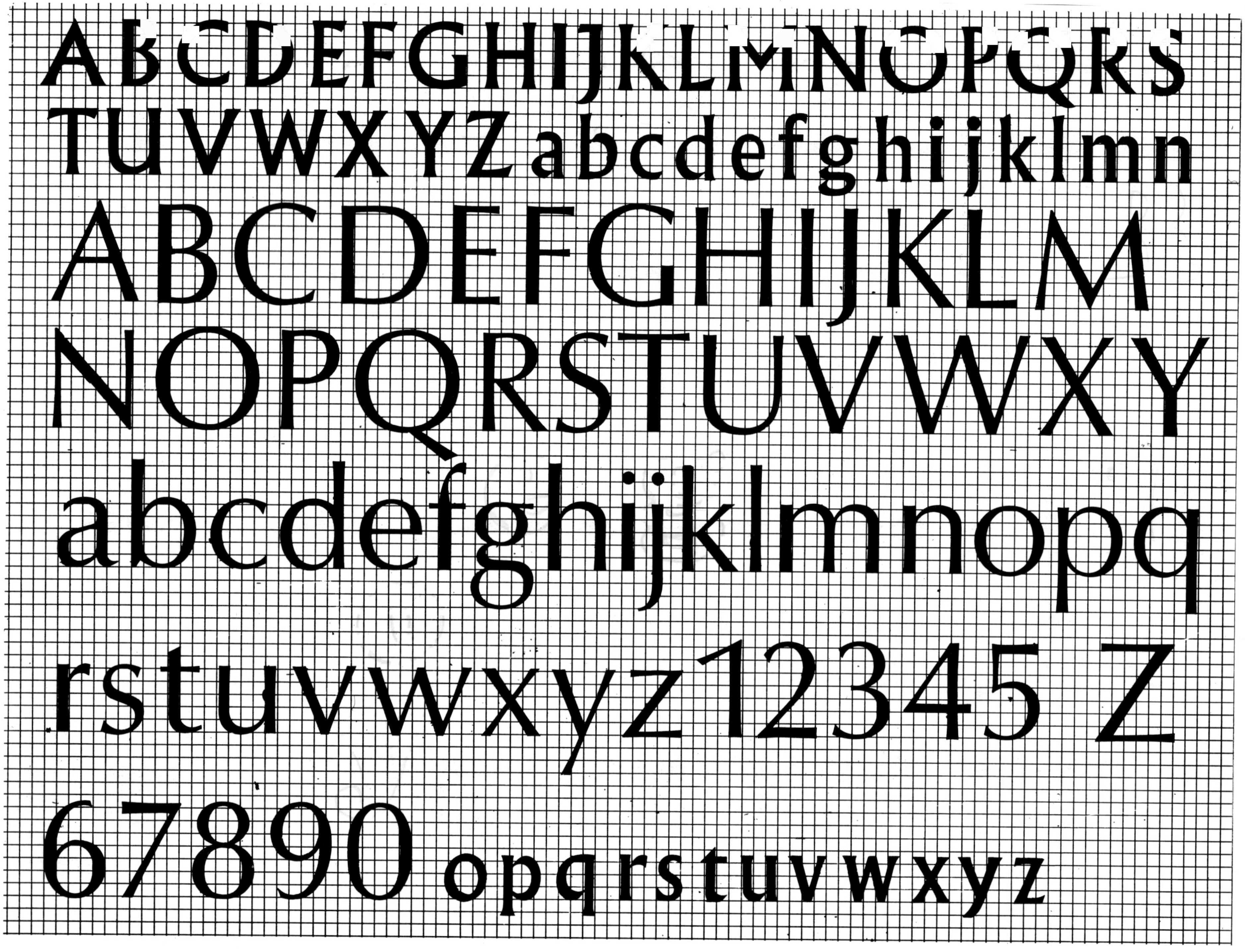
ABCDEFGHIJKLMNOPQRS
TUVWXYZ abcdefghijklmn
ABCDEFGHIJKLM
NOPQRSTUVWXY
abcdefghijklmnopq
rstuvwxyz12345 Z
67890 opqrstuvwxyz

xiv

xv

xiv   Albertus capitals and lower case
xv   Optima capitals, lower case and numerals

xvi   Clarendon Bold capitals, lower case and numerals

147

xvii   Cooper Black capitals, lower case and numerals

xviii

xix

xviii   Playbill capitals and numerals

xix   Futura Display capitals and lower case

149

ABCD
EFGHIJKL
MNOPQRS
TUVWXYZ
1234567890

abcdefg
hijklmn
opqrſst
uvwxyz

xx   Rundgotish. An attractive form of the open
gothic letter, capitals and lower case   *cf* 57 page 41

abcdefg
hijklmn
opqrst
uvwxyz

A B C D E F G

H I J J K L M N O

abcdefghijklmnopqrstuvwxyz

P Q R S T U V W

X Y Z

xxii An elegant version of the traditional copper-plate engraved letter

xxi   Unciala. Based on the early half uncial letter
cf 52 page 39

Bibliography

Lettering   Hermann Degering   *Benn*
Roman Lettering   L. C. Evetts   *Pitman*
Book of Scripts   Alfred Fairbank   *Penguin*
Lettering for Architects and Designers   Milner Gray   *Batsford*
Alphabets   Laurence Scarfe   *Batsford*
ABC of Lettering and Printing Types   Erik Lindegrin   *Museum Books New York*
Lettering   Charles R. Anderson   *Van Nostrand New York*
Lettering Techniques   John Lancaster   *Batsford*
Design with Type   Carl Dair   *University of Toronto Press*
The Art of Written Forms   Donald M. Anderson   *Holt, Rinehart and Winston*
Lettering by Modern Artists   *Museum of Modern Art New York*
Alphabet Thesaurus   Photo-Lettering Inc.   *Chapman and Hall*
The Alphabet and Elements of Lettering   Frederic W. Goudy   *Dover New York*
The Story of the Alphabet   John R. Biggs   *Oxford University Press*
Lettera I   Armin Haab and Alex Stocker   *Teufen Niggli*
Lettera II and III   Armin Haab and Walter Haettenschweiler   *Teufen Niggli*
Calligraphy Today   Heather Child   *Studio Vista*
Letraset Catalogue
Bodleian Picture Books   Bodleian Library   *Oxford University Press*
Märkbok I and II   Elsie Svennås   *ICA—Förlaget Vasteras*
Inspiration for Embroidery   Constance Howard   *Batsford*
Design in Embroidery   Kathleen Whyte   *Batsford*
The Technique of Metal Thread Embroidery   Barbara Dawson   *Batsford*
Simple Stitches   Anne Butler   *Batsford*
Stitchery: Art and Craft   Nik Krevitsky   *Reinhold New York*

Handbook of Stitches   Grete Petersen and Elsie Svennas   *Batsford*
Canvas Embroidery   Diana Springall   *Batsford*
Ideas for Canvas Work   Mary Rhodes   *Batsford*
Introducing Machine Embroidery   Ira Lillow   *Batsford*
Embroidery Stitches   Barbara Snook   *Batsford*
Filling Stitches   Edith John   *Batsford*
Creative Stitches   Edith John   *Batsford*
Making Fabric Wall Hangings   Alice Timmins   *Batsford*
The Batsford Encyclopaedia of Embroidery Stitches   Anne Butler   *Batsford*
The Constance Howard Book of Stitches   Constance Howard   *Batsford*

Suppliers in Great Britain

Nibs for lettering: script nibs

Dryad Ltd
Northgates
Leicester

Reeves Dryad Ltd
178 Kensington High Street
London W 8

Roberson and Co. Limited
77 Parkway
London NW 1

Winsor & Newton Limited
51 Rathbone Place
London W 1

*Nibs for large lettering: Boxall pens $\frac{1}{4}$ in.
to $\frac{3}{4}$ in.*

Roberson and Co. Limited
77 Parkway
London NW 1

Letraset transfer letters

Letraset Limited
195 Waterloo Road
London SE 1

Most artists' suppliers

Simplicity dressmakers' carbon paper

(for transferring patterns to fabric)
Sold in packets of assorted colours from
haberdashery departments of most large
stores

Embroidery materials

Mrs Mary Allen
Wirksworth
Derbyshire

Art Needlework Industries Limited
7 St Michael's Mansions
Ship Street
Oxford

Harrods Limited
Knightsbridge
London SW 1

I. M. Jervie
21–3 West Port
Arbroath
Tayside

John Lewis
Oxford Street
London W 1

Mace and Nairn
89 Crane Street
Salisbury
Wiltshire

The Royal School of Needlework
25 Princes Gate
South Kensington
London SW 7

The Silver Thimble
33 Gay Street
Bath
Avon

Mrs Joan Trickett
110 Marsden Road
Burnley
Lancashire

Watts and Co. Limited
7 Tufton Street
London SW 1

J. Wippell and Co. Limited
11 Tufton Street
London SW 1
55–56 High Street *and* Cathedral Yard
Exeter
24–26 King Street
Manchester

Felt and hessian

The Felt and Hessian Shop
34 Greville Street
London EC 1

Fabrics

Liberty and Co. Limited
Regent Street
London W 1

Sanderson Fabrics
56 Berners Street
London W 1

Sekers Fabrics Limited
15 Cavendish Place
London W 1

Wemyss Weavecraft Ltd
Seaforth Works
East Wemyss
Fife

Leather

R & A Kohnstamm Limited
Randack Tannery
Croydon Road
Beckenham
Kent

Weaving yarns

Campden Weavers
16 Lower High Street
Chipping Campden
Gloucestershire

T. M. Hunter Limited
Sutherland Wool Mills
Brora
Sutherland

D M C threads, etc

de Denne Limited
159/161 Kenton Road
Kenton
Harrow
Middlesex

Sewing machines

Bernina Sewing Machine Centre
Waterloo House
Lower Marsh
London SE 1

Singer Sewing Machine Co. Limited
17 Chapel Market
London N 1 *and*
334 Oxford Street
London W 1
and local branches

Sewing threads

From most departmental stores
Information about threads obtainable
from
J. and P. Coats (UK) Limited
12 Seedhill Road
PO Box 31
Paisley
Strathclyde

Suppliers in the USA

Nibs for lettering: script nibs

Stafford–Reeves Inc
626 Greenwich Street
New York NY 10014

Winsor and Newton Inc
55 Winsor Drive
Secaucus
New Jersey 07094

Embroidery materials

American Crewel Studio
Box 298 Boonton
New Jersey 07005

American Thread Corporation
90 Park Avenue
New York

Bucky King Embroideries Unlimited
Box 371, King Bros
3 Ranch Buffalo Star Rte
Sheriden
Wyoming 82801

Tinsel Trading Company
7 West 36 Street
New York NY 10018

Yarn Bazaar
Yarncrafts Limited
3146 M Street
North West Washington DC

Crewel and tapestry wool

Appleton Brothers of London
West Main Road
Little Compton
Rhode Island 02837